Unpopular

CATHOLIC

Truths

Oswald Sobrino

Editor, CatholicAnalysis.com

To John Paul II

Always Young

A Juan Pablo II

Siempre Joven

Table of Contents

FOREWORD: SOME PHILOSOPHY   5

CHAPTER ONE: ABORTION DEBATE   11

Part One: Scientific Evidence..11

Part Two: Legal Reasoning 22

CHAPTER TWO: CHASTITY AS INTEGRITY   32

CHAPTER THREE: CONTRACEPTION   42

CHAPTER FOUR: ALL-MALE PRIESTHOOD   48

CHAPTER FIVE: PETER, BISHOP OF ROME   64

CONCLUSION: THE NEW EVANGELIZATION   80

NOTES   82

BIBLIOGRAPHY   88

INDEX OF NAMES AND TOPICS   95

INDEX OF THEOLOGICAL SOURCES   99

Foreword

L et me introduce this book on Catholic truths in an unusual way by beginning with a twentieth century Spanish philosopher, little known today to the English-speaking world, who emphasized the distinction between those individuals who have a "mass" mentality and those who have a "noble" mentality. This philosopher, José Ortega y Gasset (1883-1955),* was an existentialist of sorts influenced by the philosophical currents of German universities where he received some of his advanced education.

As a typical American, I recall initially recoiling from this elitist and apparently inegalitarian distinction between the masses and noble individuals. As someone steeped in the democratic ideal, I found this part of Ortega's philosophy disturbing in spite of Ortega's protestations that his use of this distinction had nothing to do with the superiority of one social class over another.

As I grew older and more experienced, the distinction began to make more sense. Clearly,

---

* For those background materials relied upon in the following discussion of Ortega's work, see the bibliography at the end of the book.

many derive their philosophy of life uncritically from others, instead of forming their own philosophy. It reminds me of the repetitive, and often annoying, references of the German philosopher Martin Heidegger to the influential role of "they" as in "what will *they* think" or "what *they* will say."

As a Christian, I became more and more troubled by how much of my own thinking and that of others was inexorably shaped by the secular lifestyles and attitudes dyed into the very fabric of our lives. All around me traditional Christian teachings on how to live or how to seek happiness or love were treated with utter indifference, if not contempt. Even more troubling was the fact that Catholic schools and colleges exhibited virtually complete surrender to what "they" thought was normal and healthy, as opposed to what the Catholic tradition had always held to be normal and healthy.

All of which brings me back to another emphasis in Ortega's thought: the fragility of civilization. For Ortega, civilization was the result of "noble" individuals, regardless of social background, who continually challenged themselves and others with great demands and ideals. Living through the cataclysms of the twentieth century, he could see how fragile the great achievements of Western culture were when the mass mentality of totalitarianism took over, even in the cultured Germany that he knew so well.

Attempting to be a Catholic in the years after the confusion following Vatican II – a confusion, by the way, not caused by Vatican II but by the influence of outside cultural forces, I could not avoid agreeing with Ortega that the best values of civilization were indeed fragile and could virtually disappear overnight. That is why this book is about *unpopular* Catholic truths. In the modern West, the ubiquitous "they" are in favor of compassion, social justice, peace, harmony, ecological awareness, toleration, and diversity. The problem comes when it is time to translate those platitudinous commitments to concrete particular decisions.

The inspiring platitudes of our secular Western societies break down at that point. Compassion becomes a reason for abortion, for euthanasia, and for scientific research without sane limits. Social justice becomes a cover for erasing all gender distinctions, even the redefinition of marriage, at the expense of human reason. Peace becomes an idol divorced from justice and right order and devolves into emotional and escapist pacifism in the face of evil. Ecological awareness becomes the madness of embracing a vehement devotion to animal rights while at the same time proposing, in the soothing and silky tones of the academic scribbler, the killing of disabled human beings.

Like Ortega, the Spanish but non-Catholic existentialist, Catholics know that particular decisions and choices are extremely important because that is how we "make" our lives. The unpopular Catholic truths which these essays discuss challenge us to "make" or "win" our lives, as Ortega and other existentialists would say. For Ortega, living was a matter of "earning" our lives the way we earn our keep.

For Catholics, this forming of our lives through the will occurs in submission to the truth of revelation given through both Scripture and Sacred Tradition. Catholic truths are highly demanding truths. They are not popular with the mass mentality of secular elites populating the commanding cultural heights. Because of the wounded nature of our humanity, Catholic truths are highly fragile truths in the sense that they can easily slip through our fingers. These unpopular Catholic truths propose the genuinely heroic existential challenge that the twentieth century existentialists searched for but found so elusive because so many of them jettisoned belief in revelation. These truths challenge us to a genuine nobility regardless of our socio-economic origins or futures.

The following chapters are in effect essays that provide fundamental and reasoned insights into the unpopular truths of Catholicism. The authoritative declaration of these truths can be found in the *Catechism of the Catholic Church* (2nd ed. 1997). There is a brief bibliography for each chapter at the end of the book that lists relevant references to the Catechism and to other works that I have found to be helpful and reliable. The bibliographies are not superfluous boilerplate. They are invitations to form one's own insights while thinking with the mind of the Church. They are invitations for all, whether beginning with faith or without faith, to seek understanding.

Each of the following chapters treats an unpopular Catholic truth, but some of these truths are certainly not unique to Catholicism. For example, the chapter on abortion relies on scientific evidence because the startling Catholic truth about abortion is that protecting the unborn child is a human rights issue that does not depend on one's religious affiliation. Of course, Catholics also hold that there is a theological basis to protect the unborn, but that is not the only basis nor the basis required to reform our laws. Other truths focusing on sexual morality are an invitation for everyone, Catholic or not, to honor the natural use of our sexual powers.

Then there are those truths that are exclusively theological in character, such as the necessity of an all-male ministerial priesthood. Yet, even here, the Eastern Orthodox and many disgruntled Anglicans would agree with the Catholic position. Oddly enough, even some evangelicals, like the Southern Baptists, who vehemently reject even the thought of a sacramental priesthood, stubbornly cling to the idea of exclusively male senior pastors.

To add to the panorama, we also have truths that are a mixture of the historical and theological, a mixture that is present throughout the Judeo-Christian tradition, such as the truth concerning the role of Peter as the first bishop of Rome.

All of these truths together, although of varying kinds, make up the family of unpopular Catholic truths treated in this book. Some are uniquely Catholic, some are uniquely Christian in the broader sense. Some of these truths are matters of natural reason that appeal to all men and women regardless of religious identity or lack thereof. We can view these truths of natural reason as catholic with a small "c," i.e., as universal.

This description of the truths treated in this book naturally raises the question of what audience this small book is intending to address. The short answer, as you can see, is everybody: atheists, Protestants and other Christians, Jews, Moslems, agnostics. But I am also addressing my fellow Catholics for a reason that non-Catholics who are accustomed to the image of a highly disciplined and even monolithic Catholic Church might find surprising, namely, that there has been a grave and widespread collapse of clarity and orthodoxy in much of Catholic religious education and preaching in the United States which has only relatively recently shown signs of improvement. The confusion affects both the classroom and the pulpit.

For some Catholics, reading this book may be the first time they have heard a detailed defense of certain beliefs they are bound to hold as Catholics. North American Catholics, just like Western European Catholics, are embedded in highly secular cultures that view religion as dealing more with personal taste than objective truth. These secular societies view any semblance of objective truth as tied primarily to things that are quantifiable or measurable. It is a sign of the times that some of these unpopular Catholic truths may be surprising even to some Catholics. At one time, some of these truths were surprising to me.

Chapter One

Unpopular Truth No. 1: Legal Abortion is Wrong

Part One: The Scientific Evidence Against Abortion

The liberal apologist for abortion and euthanasia, legal philosopher Ronald Dworkin, opines that "the popular sense that the abortion issue is fundamentally a religious one, and some lawyers' sense that it therefore lies outside the proper limits of state action, are at bottom sound. . . ."[1] Liberal Catholic politicians hang their hat on this view: they personally oppose abortion—which, I guess, means they would not be a direct accomplice to or encourage an abortion—but just can't supposedly bring themselves to impose their personal religious belief on the nation. (Yet, some of these same liberal politicians, such as former Democratic New York governor Cuomo, are more than willing to impose their opposition to the death penalty on their fellow citizens.)

Dworkin proposes an additional constitutional basis for the abortion right in the United States: the First Amendment's clauses prohibiting the establishment of religion and protecting the free exercise of religion. Dworkin concludes that "any government that prohibits abortion commits itself to a controversial interpretation of the sanctity of life and therefore limits liberty by commanding one essentially religious position over others, which the First Amendment forbids."[2]

Yet, at bottom, the opposition to abortion is not necessarily tied to any religious convictions. The story of Dr. Bernard Nathanson is an apt illustration. He went from being a pioneer in the crusade to make abortion accessible to being a formidable pro-life activist. In his autobiographical book *The Hand of God,* Dr. Nathanson makes clear that he first became convinced of the criminality of abortion as the taking of a human life while he was an *atheist,* not because of religion but because of the scientific medical evidence. As Dr. Nathanson describes it:

> . . . . my pro-life views were scientifically based, and I made this clear to all my audiences, even the most rigidly Catholic. . . . Though pleasant and civil to the various clerics at these rallies, I made certain they knew that I held myself at a distance from their beliefs.[3]

No court, no politician, no legal commentator can ignore empirical, scientific evidence. Yet, in a society that reveres science and its measurable findings as the epitome of knowledge, there is a curious reluctance to face the scientific facts of abortion. The fact that the scientific evidence coincides with strongly held religious convictions does not justify ignoring the scientific evidence, as even Dworkin would admit.[4]

So we have the ironic situation of pro-abortion secular elites in the academy and the media retreating into obscurantism rather than facing the scientific evidence. Contrary to common perceptions, this retreat from science shows that the pro-abortion agenda is based on a primitive throwback to emotional, as opposed to scientific, reasoning. Surprisingly, it is the pro-life stance that is congruent with science and reason, while the pro-abortion advocates make a primitive appeal to the dominion of the stronger over the weaker.

The dominion of might makes right is the core of abortion advocacy, although it is phrased euphemistically as a right to privacy or to choose. It is a question of raw power and dominion, and the adults get all the power and dominion over the disposition of the unborn child. Dworkin's apologia for abortion is deceptively entitled *Life's Dominion*. A more honest title would be *Might's Dominion*.

And even more shocking than this indifference to the scientific evidence is that this evidence is not hidden away in some abstruse scientific journal: it is found in the routine ultrasound experienced by expectant mothers throughout the country in order to monitor gestational age and development of the unborn child and to even disclose, when requested by the parents, the gender of the unborn child. It is exposure to ultrasound pictures of the fetus being aborted that turned a hardened, pioneering, and prominent abortionist like Dr. Nathanson into a pro-life activist.

The ultrasound is high-tech, visual, and irrefutable evidence that the fetus is a baby inside the womb. We are not talking about a legal fiction or concept or argument. We are talking about live pictures of a live baby developing in the womb. All the armchair spinning and legal analogies fall flat in the face of this scientific evidence.

What does the ultrasound of an abortion show us? It shows the brutal dismembering of a developing child.[5] It shows the unborn child thrashing about reflexively as the physician attacks with the tools of abortion.[6] The visual evidence shows a small, developing human being who just happens to be growing in the womb, rather than outside the womb. The evidence shows the killing of a human being.

The abortion apologists try to get around this self-evident killing by arguing that there is no evidence that the fetus feels pain or is aware of pain. But, of course, no one really knows whether or not pain is felt; it remains an open question. In fact, the question of pain remains an abstract, philosophical issue focusing on how much awareness corresponds to "feeling pain." The only reasonable approach to take is to presume that some degree of pain is felt in the course of a brutal attack to which the human being is obviously responding with rapid thrashing movements to escape the attack.

Yet, as Nathanson points out, the question of pain is beside the point. A developing human being is still a human being. Contemporary philosophers emphasize the continuities of life and nature as opposed to a mechanistic understanding of a ghostly soul inhabiting a machine-like body. Yet, that outdated mechanistic conception is what the abortionists propose. They propose that the body as it appears in the ultrasound is irrelevant to the personhood of the fetus. The abortionists focus on awareness and consciousness because the physical evidence is undeniable. By doing so, the abortion defenders evoke a split between mind and body.

The more reasonable approach is to recognize that the obviously human form in the ultrasound is concomitantly developing human consciousness. The two go hand in hand. Again, the irony is that the secular abortionists rely on a ghostly, ambiguous, and indefinable concept of consciousness, while the anti-abortion position relies on the straightforward physical evidence of continuous development.

The ultrasounds have revolutionized embryology and fetology.[7] In a culture saturated with abortion, expectant mothers are told every detail of the developments in the womb. One book published as a popular guide for expectant mothers unambiguously lists the milestones. At a gestational age of 2 weeks, the critical five week phase for heart and central nervous system development begins.[8] At the age of 4 weeks, the heart begins to beat.[9] At the age of 5 weeks, the "nervous system is beginning to develop and spontaneously moves . . . [the] muscles."[10] At the age of 8 weeks, well within the first trimester, all organs have been formed.[11]

On and on the process goes, methodically and inevitably. And it is a process that is quintessentially measurable in a way that fits the standards of a scientific culture. And also remember that the above-mentioned milestones are an incomplete sample of what is already happening in the *first trimester.* These descriptions of the developmental milestones are intentionally taken from a book mass marketed to pregnant women to show that the rapid pace of embryonic development in the first trimester is not some secret for experts only. The abortion culture and the ultrasound culture are in deep contradiction and conflict. And that contradiction is in plain view of all Americans.

Yet, the impact of these facts is even greater the more one looks closely at the medical evidence. As Dr. John Collins Harvey, Professor of Medicine at Georgetown University Medical Center, succinctly puts it: "By the ninth week of gestation, the embryo has developed into a fetus, which in appearance resembles a miniature adult."[12] Again, at nine weeks, you are still in the first trimester in which *Roe v. Wade* forbids any state regulation of abortion.

One landmark and detailed medical publication that visually captures what the new technology can show us about the developing unborn child is aptly entitled *An Atlas of the Human Embryo and Fetus: A Photographic Review of Human Prenatal Development.*[13] In the foreword to the atlas, Prof. Louis G. Keith, M.D., of Northwestern University Medical School, states that "this Atlas is destined to become a classic landmark in the field of embryology and an invaluable addition to our specialty."[14] Here we have a medical text in the specialty of embryology that has no trace of any partisanship on the abortion issue. It is an exclusively scientific tome focusing on observation and measurement. Yet, the visual impact of the atlas is unmistakable: now the naked human eye can see the unborn child in great detail quite early in its development.

One detailed photo of a 29-day-old embryo already distinctly shows the concave curvature of the body.[15] To the layman's eyes, at 47 to 48 days, an amazing embryo is present "with a distinct face and eyes without eyelids," with primitive fingers and toes.[16] By 57 days, the photos show a tiny baby.[17] The editor of the atlas comments that the "early fetus appears fully human" in describing a photo from the 13th gestational week.[18]

Finally, a stunning and troubling photograph of a fetus aborted in the 21st gestational week in the second trimester is visually indistinguishable from a full term baby.[19] Add to all of this abundant scientific evidence the fact that forty days from conception the brain waves of the fetus can be measured.[20] The facts of very early significant development of the unborn child are for the most part undisputed. As they say in courtrooms, the parties can stipulate to the evidence.

Thus, with meticulous scientific precision, the humanity of the unborn child is manifested in a way that only the most hardened ideologue can ignore. Here is the great contradiction of legalized abortion: as time goes on, more and more visual scientific evidence contradicts the legal ruling that the embryo and fetus are not persons entitled to the same protection as the full term infant. The legal superstructure supporting abortion continues to develop an ever-widening crack caused by a science that unceasingly progresses in its efforts to document fetal life in powerful visual images that can speak directly to the general public.

This crack is now a chasm. American constitutional jurisprudence is in direct conflict with the advances of science. I submit that this conflict is unsustainable. In the end, either the jurisprudence must admit that it is legalizing infanticide or reverse *Roe v. Wade.* Just as in the era when Lincoln said that a house divided against itself over slavery cannot stand, so today a nation whose legal theories and continually growing scientific evidence are in blatant contradiction cannot stand.

Both intellectually and practically, American law, like any other legal system, ought to be a coherent web of interdependent concepts. Concepts such as the "reasonable man" standard in criminal, contract and personal injury law consistently reappear in different areas of legal practice. Other concepts are less explicit but nevertheless widespread, such as the rationale of minimizing economic transaction costs that supports case law in many different areas, from the obvious commercial applications to less obvious applications in the area of personal injury law. Other concepts that cut across the legal landscape include forseeability, causation, and freedom of association. Yet, there is a fundamental core concept that underlies the entire legal field: human dignity.

In the criminal law, human dignity requires a presumption of innocence and proof beyond a reasonable doubt. In contract law, human dignity requires remedies to protect those at a disadvantage in bargaining power or those who have detrimentally and reasonably relied on a promise that has been broken. In tort (personal injury) law, human dignity requires that third parties be able to recover from manufacturers who have made defective products, even if there is no direct relationship between the injured person and the manufacturer. In constitutional law, human dignity permeates any discussion of rights. And, of course, human dignity makes sense only when predicated of a human person. Thus, personhood lies at the basis of much of our legal superstructure.

Consequently, defining personhood in effect defines the entire field of American law. When the Supreme Court allows the state to ignore personhood prior to viability and even thereafter, it has redefined the keystone of American law. The abortion case law denies personhood to a child who is dependent: the child in the womb. All else is the same. In or out of the womb, we have human life. The only difference is a traditional, almost atavistic, and primitive attachment to the notion that being *in utero* renders the child a chattel of the mother. The raw power used to strip personhood from the unborn child lacks any intellectual underpinning.

The current abortion jurisprudence basically says that the mother can do with the unborn child what she wishes since the child is physiologically dependent on her. Even more striking in its arbitrariness is the Supreme Court's reasoning that because people have become accustomed to expecting abortion on demand the Court's hands are now tied. Nothing is more difficult to believe than that the same Supreme Court that boldly invalidated the anti-abortion laws of states throughout the union back in 1973 cannot bring itself to disappoint the settled expectations of today's society. It is even more difficult to believe that the Supreme Court's hands are tied when you see the same Supreme Court striking down sodomy laws in a way that sets the stage to redefine the marriage laws of the entire nation in a revolutionary manner.

By an exercise of raw judicial power, with precious little rational substance in support, the Supreme Court has undermined the core concept of American law: human dignity. Individual human dignity is now tied to the concept of independence. Any dependent human life, whether an unborn child or a disabled child or an elderly person, is now in the danger zone. This new legal zone is a danger zone where the protections of citizenship do not apply.

The analogy drawn by pro-life forces to the infamous pre-Civil War *Dred Scott* decision is apt. In *Dred Scott,* the Supreme Court denied personhood to persons of African descent and thus excluded them from constitutional protection. This denial of personhood tore the union apart. Lincoln famously noted—by quoting the Gospel— that a house divided against itself cannot stand. Once again, the Supreme Court has badly served and divided the nation by denying personhood to obvious persons.

What are the consequences of such a dreadful exercise of judicial power? Will there be another civil war? In a way, there is another civil war already underway. It has become common to talk of culture wars. These culture wars have divided the country in half. The results of the 2000 presidential election show a fundamental split in the nation between social conservatism and social liberalism. Abortion is the key cultural divide. As science continues to expose the gruesomeness of abortion, much as abolitionist literature like *Uncle Tom's Cabin* exposed the cruelty of slavery, the ability of more and more Americans to look the other way on abortion is eroded.

Part Two

The Legal Reasoning Behind the Abortion Right in the United States

The reasoning behind the Supreme Court decisions upholding the right to abort the unborn child is part of a specific type of reasoning normally unfamiliar to non-lawyers. I will evaluate the reasoning in the two most significant abortion cases: obviously, *Roe v. Wade* (1973), and the lesser known but crucial *Planned Parenthood v. Casey* (1992). What will become apparent is that the legal reasoning in each decision completely ignores the scientific evidence in blatant contradiction to the twentieth century trend in American law to carefully consider new factual developments underlying any legal issue. Examples of such legally relevant factual developments include the hardships of child labor in factories, the inequities in segregated school systems, and the economics of imposing certain transaction or economic costs on particular parties.

This trend in legal reasoning has progressive and liberal roots as part of the effort to have courts uphold social reform. The same trend is also evident in conservative attempts to have courts recognize the economic consequences of government regulation. Yet, the two landmark abortion decisions, especially the later 1992 decision that we will discuss, fail to engage the scientific and social facts underlying the abortion debate.

The lengthy *Roe v. Wade* decision can be reduced to three important holdings:

1. Prior to the approximate end of the first trimester, "the abortion . . . decision must be left to the medical judgment of the pregnant woman's attending physician."[21]
2. After the approximate end of the first trimester, "the State . . . may . . . regulate the abortion procedure in ways that are reasonably related to maternal health."[22]
3. Finally, "subsequent to viability the State, in promoting its interests in the potentiality of human life, may, if it chooses, regulate, and even proscribe, abortion except where necessary, in appropriate medical judgment, for the preservation of the life or health of the mother."[23]

As you can see from the third holding listed above, the edifice of *Roe* is built on the factual, scientific issue of viability. The unstated philosophical premise is that the ability to live independently of the body of the mother is a prerequisite to the right to life. In other words, dependency implies that the mother has the power of life and death over the unborn child.

This logic of dependency is now being extended by philosophers and legislators to more and more areas: the dependent disabled infant, the dependent terminally ill patient, the dependent elderly person. In all these circumstances, the dependent human life becomes less than a person. The comparison with chattel slavery which viewed the black slave as non-human property is chillingly apt. The fetus or the disabled or other burdensome dependent is at the mercy of those who have an economic obligation to care for the dependent.

This fundamental notion of dependency as a distinguishing trait of the non-person is easily amenable to an economic and monetary framework. If the child is allowed to be born, then the mother will be unduly burdened due to her poverty, or due to her need to care for other children, or due to the disruption of her career and educational plans. The famously amorphous phrase "health of the mother" encompasses the emotional distress, or disutility as the economists would say, arising from the burden of a born child. Again, we have the dependent human being treated as an economic asset, as in the case of black slavery in the nineteenth century.

In the case of the elderly and debilitated person, the economic burden falls on relatives or the government or both. The logic is simple and clear: all those bearing part of this economic burden have an interest in deciding the fate of the dependent. That economic logic of dependency is very appealing to a highly utilitarian American culture which is predisposed to expand its applicability to more and more life situations in American society. The powerful hold of economic reasoning on American culture and law bodes well for the continued flourishing of this depersonalizing logic. But, of course, this logic bodes ill for human rights.

In spite of this dehumanizing result, in 1992, the Court in *Planned Parenthood v. Casey* specifically reaffirmed viability as the key to its abortion jurisprudence because "the concept of viability . . . is the time at which there is a realistic possibility of maintaining and nourishing a life outside the womb, so that the **independent** existence of the second life can, in reason and all fairness, be the object of state protection that now overrides the rights of the woman" (emphasis added).[24]

If that logic is to be dethroned, the notion of dependency as depersonalizing must be jettisoned. What can replace it? Contrary to the straw man argument advanced by pro-abortion activists, no religious argument is needed. The clear biological fact of new life—notice, I did not use the Court's euphemism "potential for human life"—is a non-arbitrary and scientifically verifiable basis for defining a human person.

It is indisputable that a new and different human life begins at conception. The issue is when we will bestow personhood and its attendant rights on that new human life. The Supreme Court offers the outdated and scientifically irrelevant concept of viability, while science, with its discovery of the genetic code that controls human life in detail, offers us conception or fertilization as that point in time when personhood has literally been determined. At fertilization, the chromosomes are in place. All else is development along a continuum. At fertilization, new life is determined in all its detail. There is no scientific basis for postponing personhood to the point of viability.

In addition, defining personhood at fertilization does not rely on the dependency argument and its economic reductionism of human life. Personhood at fertilization is an idea based on a clear-cut biological event that is scientifically unassailable. Personhood at fertilization does not depend on any extraneous philosophical or religious assumptions, while the personhood, or at least limited personhood, imposed by the Court at viability is scientifically arbitrary and stems from the arbitrary equating of dependency with non-personhood.

The choice is between a scientific and non-arbitrary definition of personhood proposed by the pro-life movement and a highly subjective and economistic equating of personhood with independence as proposed by the Supreme Court.

As in much of American law, until the advent of the economic analysis of law by such scholars as Posner, the economic logic in *Roe v. Wade* remained hidden behind florid language about privacy and fundamental rights and liberty. Neither privacy nor liberty requires equating the right to life with viability. Only the economic logic of burdensome dependency requires this unscientific demarcation between totally disposable human life and human life subject to state protection.

Even more significantly, using viability to indicate the independent existence that justifies state protection is self-contradictory. Even a viable infant is dependent on the mother for his existence. And, of course, every child, whether premature or full-term, remains dependent for years and years on parental care. As a result, the Court's focus on independent existence as the criterion for protection of human life can be easily brushed aside as nonsensical by those wishing to remove any restrictions at all on abortion. The inability of the independent life criterion to protect human life at all is plainly evident in the arguments of those who argue for the killing of disabled infants or for adult euthanasia. The rationale of independent existence cannot fulfill the function of protecting any life because all lives depend at some point on the care of others.

The internal contradiction of the Court's abortion jurisprudence can only be removed by rejecting the identification of personhood with independent existence. Yet, what else can the Court substitute to justify protecting an unborn child after so many weeks, but not earlier? There is no logical place for the Court to go. The ultimate logical outcome of the Court's present line of abortion cases is complete abortion on demand regardless of viability. To provide any state protection for the unborn child will ultimately require abandoning viability as the critical boundary and substituting fertilization.

At conception or fertilization, we have a new and different life. Fertilization as the point of state protection does not depend on the extraneous assumption that protected life must somehow be "independent." State protection at fertilization means that every new life must be protected by the state. Personhood is a mark of every new and different life. This new point of state protection has the advantages of clarity, simplicity, freedom from extraneous philosophical or religious assumptions, and, most importantly, continuing objective validation by modern science.

Yet, the Court refuses to take this necessary step to correct the scientifically baseless and arbitrary reasoning of *Roe v. Wade.* Not only is the refusal to correct this case law inconsistent with the scientific evidence but it also contradicts conventional descriptions of legal reasoning. In Edward Levi's classic book *An Introduction to Legal Reasoning,* the author takes note of how jurisprudence develops in American law by discussing examples from tort and constitutional law. One example he develops at length is the expansion of the tort or personal injury liability of merchants to third parties by expanding the concept of "things dangerous in themselves" to include more and more new products.[25]

Levi summarizes this change in legal reasoning:

> The liability of a seller of a previously innocuous article was not enlarged

because some economic theory said this would be appropriate. Rather the growth of inventions made it hard to distinguish, when reasoning by example was used, between steam engines thought unusual and dangerous in an early day, and engines that moved and were now commonplace [that is, cars].[26]

Likewise, today's abortion case law must expand legally protected personhood to include the new data and graphic images made possible by advancing science. Applying reasoning by example to the fetus requires recognizing that a new and different human life is present long before the point of viability. The presence of a different genetic code, plus the rapid development of organs, the ability to move, and the early detection of brain waves make the point of viability irrelevant. And, as shown earlier, the point of viability is in reality an arbitrary choice because there is no true independent life even after viability. The viable child, the born child, the growing child will remain dependent on parental care for years.

Yet, in *Casey,* the Court showed an odd reluctance to reverse *Roe v. Wade:*

> [W]hile the effect of reliance on *Roe* cannot be exactly measured, neither can the certain cost of overruling *Roe* for people who have ordered their thinking and living around that case be dismissed.[27]

This reluctance defies Levi's conventional, if not liberal, views of constitutional reasoning:

> In addition to the power to hold legislative acts invalid, a written constitution confers another and perhaps as great a power. It is the power to disregard prior cases. . . . The problem of *stare decisis* where a constitution is involved is therefore an entirely different matter from that in case law or legislation. . . . A change of mind from time to time is inevitable when there is a written constitution. . . . It [the Court] can always abandon what has been said in order to go back to the written document itself.[28]

"Stare decisis" is the Latin legal term for the rule that courts should follow their prior decisions or precedent. What Levi says is that in constitutional matters courts can abandon their prior decisions by going back to the state or federal constitution itself. Thus, the Supreme Court is free to abandon the arbitrary and self-contradictory viability standard of *Roe* by going back to the Constitution's protection of personal liberty on the basis of new scientific evidence establishing the personhood of the unborn child from the time of fertilization. If legal precedent has been abandoned on other more mundane issues, it certainly can be abandoned when it comes to state protection of human life.

The Supreme Court's reluctance to reverse *Roe v. Wade* stands in the face of contradicting

scientific evidence and in the face of an arbitrary and nonsensical focus on viability. The
Court's rhetoric thus becomes a cover for the
raw exercise of power by adults over dependent
human life for the sake of adult personal con-
venience. This rhetoric is discredited by both
science and logic, and cannot even rely on conventional views of constitutional reasoning to
withstand the necessity of its abandonment.

Chapter Two

Unpopular Truth No. 2: Chastity is Personal Integrity

I f you look up "chastity" in *Webster's Ninth New Collegiate Dictionary,* two basic definitions are given. The first definition gives the expected meaning: "abstention from unlawful sexual intercourse." But what I am interested in pursuing in this chapter is the second definition which is rarely heard in our modern society: chastity as "personal integrity."

I recall one writer in the liberal periodical *Commonweal* complaining that he could not understand why so much was made of Pope John Paul's theology of the body. In his view, the Pope's work failed to address the positive aspects of sexuality and sexual pleasure. His comments are another confirmation that even highly educated and otherwise perceptive writers fail to see what is before their very eyes. To someone trying to understand the Pope's theology of the body, I would point to Webster's second definition quoted above: personal integrity.

In our current modern Western societies, we are beset with protests about the lack of

personal integrity of corporations, public offi-
cials, religious leaders, and other notables that
is regularly exposed by the investigative media.
The modern emphasis, at least in the United
States, is on truthful disclosures whether by
nominees to government office or corporations
making stock offerings. In addition, environ-
mentalists demand to know the full impact of
new projects on natural resources. Exposé after
exposé tries to uncover supposedly secret scan-
dalous behavior. Of late, the Catholic Church
has been an especially attractive target,
whether it is speculation about action or inac-
tion during the Holocaust or about transferring
sexual abusers from parish to parish.

Yet, there is a deafening silence about the
personal demands of *individual* integrity. According to the Catholic Church, personal integrity demands chastity. Not surprisingly, the
secular media does not pursue this point. Yet,
journalists are supposed to be paragons of personal integrity pursuing the unrighteous. Interestingly some journalists, like former CBS cor-
respondent Bernard Goldberg, have documented the bias that is endemic in much of the
media—a bias that is itself a failure of personal
integrity. The plain truth is that most secular
journalists are not going to write about chastity
as personal integrity even if a news story is
bursting with the relevance of chastity as personal integrity.

Recall coverage of President Clinton's blatant sexual exploitation of the twenty-
something intern in the White House. The man-
tra from the media and most Democrats was

that this exploitation was private and irrelevant to the conduct of his presidential duties. The focus instead was on the legal issues of perjury and obstruction of justice. While I agree that the perjury and obstruction of justice issues were certainly relevant (and, in my opinion, worthy of conviction at the Senate impeachment trial), the more fundamental, threshold issue was character: the lack of personal integrity made plain by the sexual exploitation. Lack of chastity reveals lack of personal integrity. Just ask a betrayed boyfriend or girlfriend, fiancé or spouse.

Once we adopt this realistic and hardnosed view of chastity, lack of chastity is no longer quite as dashing, mischievous, excusable, or "normal" as we usually like to make it out to be. We all know that the effects of lack of personal integrity are wide-ranging and seriously destructive. Thus, the Catholic Church, and not only the Catholic Church, views lack of chastity as having seriously destructive consequences on the participants themselves and on the rest of society.

Yet, the Pope's analysis in his work on the theology of the body does not focus in utilitarian fashion on consequences alone, and rightly so, since an emphasis on consequences easily leads to a moral relativism that is foreign to the moral teaching of the Catholic Church. Let us take a closer look at the Pope's theology of the body.

In my opinion, the key to understanding the Pope's explanation of traditional Catholic teaching on chastity brings us right back to the dictionary definition: personal integrity. For the Pope, we must view lack of chastity as a "lie" in order to understand its dehumanizing and anti-human message. So, in the end, the commandments that in Catholic tradition specifically call us to chaste behavior, the sixth and ninth commandments on adultery and coveting your neighbor's wife, are from this point of view applications of another broader commandment: "Thou shall not bear false witness against thy neighbor."

Chastity is desirable in itself because truthful witness about oneself and one's neighbor is intrinsically desirable as a matter of personal integrity. Fornication, adultery, and other expressions of lack of chastity are intrinsically evil for the same reason that a lie is intrinsically evil: it is not consistent with our personal integrity as rational and dignified human beings. Catholics and other theists would add that this human dignity derives from our creation in the image and likeness of God. Yet, this analysis of chastity is intelligible even to the atheist or agnostic who believes in the inherent dignity of human beings.

The link between lack of chastity and lack of integrity is evident in a seldom used English word: "meretricious." The word derives from the Latin *meretrix* meaning "prostitute."[29] The dictionary still lists this original meaning as current and defines meretricious as "having the nature of prostitution."[30] But the same dictionary also gives the meanings that usually come first to the minds of most of us: "tawdrily and falsely attractive" or "pretentious." Most of us think of a meretricious statement or writing as false and deceptive.

Of course, that is the nature of prostitution itself which falsifies the central meaning of the sexual act as radical mutual commitment. And so we say that an artist who descends to tawdry commercialism has "prostituted" himself, or that the politician who deserts his ideals for campaign contributions has "prostituted" himself. In both cases, we sense that the artist or the public servant has become a liar by his very behavior.

In this sense, unchaste behavior is likewise meretricious because it debases the genuine meaning of the sexual act as an inherently marital act. Without the commitment of marriage, the sexual act is set loose from its truth and becomes a tawdry spectacle much like the commercialized artist or the corrupt politician. It becomes a debasement full of dishonor.

In this era of social engineering by activist courts, we must also add that, when we say that the sexual act is inherently a marital act, Catholic and biblical teaching presumes the complementary union of male and female. The obvious natural end and integrity of our sexual powers are ordered to procreation. To pretend otherwise is, well, pretense. It is meretricious. The procreative potential of the sexual union of male and female is intrinsic to the radical nature of the commitment signified by the sexual act.

Catholics and other Christians affirm the truth that our bodies are just as much part of our identity as our souls. Persons are composites of body and soul. In the drama of procreation, we see clearly the personal unity of body and soul in which biology reflects the radical nature of the marital commitment. Without that procreative potential, which is biologically inscribed in our natures, the sexual act becomes a lie and a pretense. There can be no genuine marital act between those of the same gender. So when we say that chastity is a matter of personal integrity, we should realize that "personal" refers not just to the soul but also to the natural biological integrity of our bodies. In sexuality, personal integrity includes natural integrity.

With this focus on integrity, chastity stops being the sort of "cowardly" or effeminate virtue that is vaguely alien to the average red-blooded male. In this regard, we must also add that many women today view "chastity" as somehow oppressive or contrary to their personal fulfillment. But once chastity becomes a matter of fundamental personal integrity, it is once again identified as a true virtue worthy of strong-willed and mature men and women who refuse to debase themselves. That is the vision missed by the unsatisfied *Commonweal* writer. That is the vision of John Paul II's theology of the body.

The theology of the body enables us to give a direct answer to the fundamental question: why is sexual activity outside of marriage a lie? For that we must take a more detailed look at the Pope's work. John Paul begins his development of the theology of the body with the biblical creation account. He goes back to

Genesis to find the original meaning of gender or sex: man, created as male and female. In all of his teaching, his intent is to give a personalistic explanation of the truth of human sexuality. With this personalistic intent, he is determined to explain the truth about sexuality in direct relation to the dignity of the human person created in the image of God.

The Pope begins his analysis of Genesis by pointing out that the "creation of man consists in the creation of the unity of two beings."[31] This unity is "an overcoming of the frontier of solitude" which leads to a communion of persons.[32] The "very core" of this reality is the human body which reveals the common humanity of man and woman.[33] The body in its male and feminine forms expresses the truth that male and female are a mutual gift to each other.[34] This complementarity is why the meaning of marriage requires a union of male and female.

The Pope calls this truth about the human body the "nuptial meaning" of the body.[35] This nuptial meaning is "the capacity of expressing love, that love in which the person becomes a gift – and by means of this gift – fulfills the meaning of his being and existence."[36] John Paul hearkens back to the Second Vatican Council's declaration "that man 'can fully discover his true self only in a sincere giving of himself.'"[37]

In this mutual gift, the man and the woman affirm each other as created by God: the male as created by God "for his own sake" and the female as likewise created by God "for her own sake."[38] By the phrase "for his or her own sake," the Pope means that each "person is unique and unrepeatable, someone chosen by eternal Love."[39] The permanent commitment of marriage, whose divine origin is recounted in Genesis, is the arena for this mutual gift to the unique and unrepeatable other.

When humans deviate from this complementary marital communion of unique and unrepeatable persons through mutual self-giving, what emerges is lust or concupiscence. Lust "depersonalizes man making him an object 'for the other.'"[40] The result is that "the relationship of the gift is changed into the relationship of appropriation."[41] Consequently, the use of bodies as means of depersonalized appropriation falsifies and contradicts the nuptial meaning of the body. Lack of chastity is a lie about the human body. Lack of chastity lies by declaring that the other exists to be used as an object.

The conclusion is that sexual activity outside the full mutual self-giving of marriage is the perpetration of a lie that contradicts the fact that man, both male and female, was created by God for his own sake. To be more blunt, lack of chastity is lack of personal integrity because it lies about our bodies, our dignity, and our origins. That's the basis of the Catholic teaching about chastity. As you can see, its basis is intelligible to all, whether Catholic or not, who believe in God's creation of unique but complementary persons endowed with dignity. It is even intelligible to atheists who believe in human dignity. The Catholic position is not fundamentally about repression or denial. The unpopular Catholic truth about chastity is that it is about your personal integrity.

In our modern Western societies, this link between integrity and chastity has long been forgotten. You get a whiff now and then when even secular feminists become alarmed over the frequency of date rape and other forms of rape or about the brutal pornography that specializes in the victimization of women. You see instances of disquiet in the secular realm when the dark results of the abandonment of chastity are starkly exposed by some disturbing incident. Yet, the concern expressed over the exploitation of women issues in no solution because the preconceived analysis of such problems excludes considerations of chastity.

The secular West is intent on attempting the creation of a non-exploitative world combined with a world that recognizes very little in the way of limits on sexual behavior. That combination is doomed to failure. A non-exploitative world requires an anchor for human dignity. Catholics propose that human beings have a unique dignity rooted in their distinctive capacity to reason which reflects the intelligent designer of the universe. With such an anchor, human dignity is secure. Without any such anchor, the secular project for a non-exploitative society will fail because it has no fixed standard by which to veto the expression of new and old forms of exploitation.

Can non-theists find such a reliable anchor for human dignity? Personally, I don't see how.

Any anchor for human dignity must be authoritative and demand submission to a certain truth. The secular disavowal of any certain moral truths valid for all emasculates any secular project for human dignity.

The most extreme example of secularism's catastrophic failure to secure human dignity was Communism. Rejecting any divine anchor for human dignity, the communists ended up breaking every moral rule devised by man ostensibly for the sake of human dignity. Starvation, massacres, torture, separation of families, prison camps became the tools of building a better social order. To attempt to base human dignity on mere secular values is to build a house on sand, as described in the gospel parable.

In the end, the call to chastity is a call for the truthful use of our bodies. The truth of the human body is that it was made to express the full gift of self to someone of the opposite and complementary gender. The arena for such expression is what the Church and most of mankind still call marriage.

Chapter Three

Unpopular Truth No. 3: The Marital Act is Open to Life

G iven that chastity is personal integrity, there comes a point when personal integrity demands sexual union. As we have seen, the only arena where personal integrity demands sexual union is in the full commitment of marriage. It is now a commonplace that most Catholics reject the Church's teaching that to attempt to prevent conception while engaging in the marital act is a grave sin. (Please note that by "marital act" I am referring to the full sexual union of male and female by which we reproduce.)

That commonplace must be qualified, however. Within the Catholic Church, many religious educators, whether lay or clerical, have simply refused to communicate what the Church teaches. And even when unsympathetically communicated, the teaching is presented with a nod and a wink using that great loophole: follow your conscience. But the Catholic tradition teaches that the conscience you are required to follow must be an informed conscience and that voluntary ignorance or indifference is morally culpable.

The educators who reject the Church position on contraception intentionally refuse to inform consciences and then have the audacity to recommend that their listeners follow their duly uninformed consciences. So if polls or surveys or anecdotal experiences show that many Catholics reject the teaching, we must be careful to remember that few Catholics have ever heard the teaching presented sympathetically and intelligently. But what many Catholics do hear from governments, schools, television, books, radio, and the internet is that contraception is an innocuous and even necessary part of sexual relations. No less can be expected from a culture that views sex as a casual recreation or as a form of social introduction.

That is why this chapter on birth control must follow the chapter on chastity. If you reject chastity, then certainly any limits on birth control are nonsensical. If you accept fornication with birth control, you would find absurd that, all of a sudden, within marriage you must completely forego birth control. That is why, in my view, the central issue in the debate about birth control is the question of chastity. If the parties to a debate fail to agree on the value of chastity, they are doomed to disagreement on the subject of birth control.

In addition, the birth control mentality is logically and realistically tied to the abortion mentality treated in the first chapter. John Paul II has noted this self-evident link between abortion and birth control in his encyclical *The Gospel of Life* (known also by its Latin name *Evangelium Vitae*) when he says that "[d]espite their differences of nature and moral gravity, contraception and abortion are often closely connected, as fruits of the same tree."[42] The Pope makes note of the iron triangle of fornication, contraception, and abortion, all linked to sustain a "hedonistic mentality."[43] The result is that "abortion becomes the only possible decisive response to failed contraception."[44]

Professor Janet Smith of Detroit's Sacred Heart Major Seminary has written widely in defense of the Church's teaching on contraception and has noted how even the U.S. Supreme Court, in a decision we have already examined when discussing legal abortion, has recognized that legal abortion is a necessary safety net for failed contraception. The Supreme Court has stated that *Roe v. Wade* should not be overruled because "for two decades of economic and social developments, people have organized intimate relationships and made choices that define their views of themselves and their places in society, *in reliance on the availability of abortion in the event that contraception should fail*" (emphasis added).[45] The Supreme Court itself, certainly far from a Catholic or Christian venue, has made the link for all to see.

In the end, the Church urges that we keep the marital act open to new life because that is what personal integrity demands. It is now unfashionable, even in some Catholic circles, to say that the central aim or end of marriage is the procreation and education of children. Some will even point to Vatican II and say that the Church no longer technically ranks the traditional ends or aims of marriage as it used to do.

Well, let us put quibbles aside and see what the Council said about marriage and children in the document *Gaudium et Spes:* "By their very nature, the institution of matrimony itself and conjugal love are ordained for the procreation and education of children, and find in them their ultimate crown."[46] Children are the "crown" of marriage. We are already deep into a world view radically different from that of the secular, affluent West in which, in spite of all our relative affluence, children, especially when they number more than two, are increasingly viewed as burdens rather than crowns.

This viewpoint is so fundamental to the Council that it is repeated almost verbatim in a later section of the same document: "Marriage and conjugal love are by their nature ordained toward the begetting and educating of children. Children are really the supreme gift of marriage and contribute very substantially to the welfare of their parents" (*Gaudium et Spes,* 50).

The Council continues:

> Hence, while not making the other purposes of matrimony of less account, the true practice of conjugal love and the whole meaning of family life which results from it have this aim: that the couple be ready with stout hearts to cooper-

ate with the love of the Creator and of the Savior, who through them will enlarge and enrich his own family day by day (*Gaudium et Spes*, 50).

Some will say that in Vatican II the Church elevated the marital friendship of the spouses to a level of parity with the aim of procreation. Many of these arguments will view St. Augustine's traditional listing of the goods involved in marriage (the goods of offspring, fidelity, and indissolubility) as somehow being altered by the Council.

In my view, the Council did not engage in any such revisionism. Rather, the Council represented the traditional teaching on marriage in a more integrated way so that the conjugal love or friendship of the spouses could be better seen for modern eyes as inseparable from the goods of offspring, fidelity, and indissolubility. The words quoted above are clear. The aim or end of conjugal love is procreation. Conjugal love is inherently ordained to the end of procreation. And procreation becomes the crowning expression of conjugal love.

Children are the ultimate incarnation of conjugal love. For Catholics, this view of children is easy to understand because we hold that God who is love became flesh in the child Jesus, born of the Virgin Mary.

A lucid resolution of this debate comes from the pen of John Paul II before he became pope. Under his pre-papal name of Karol Wojtyla, the Pope begins his analysis by listing the three traditional aims of marriage: the primary end of procreation, the mutual help given by the spouses to each other, and the satisfaction of sexual desire.[47]

But he also makes use of the "personalistic norm" which asserts that the "only proper and adequate way to relate" to a person is through love.[48] He argues that this personalistic norm of love is the principle upon which each of the three aims of marriage must be realized.[49]

Thus, procreation is not separable from love and cannot conflict with love. He goes on to write that the three aims of marriage, understood in this personalistic manner, can "only be realized in practice as a single complex aim."[50] There is no rivalry between conjugal love and the primary aim of procreation.

From the words of Vatican II to the allegedly controversial teaching of Paul VI in his encyclical *Humanae Vitae,* which in 1968 reaffirmed the traditional prohibition of birth control, the path is clear and easy. For in 1968, Paul VI merely reaffirmed that the marital act must always preserve that unity of conjugal love and procreation, or, as he termed it, the unitive and procreative dimensions of the marital act.

Given the howls of dissent that greeted the issuance of the encyclical, one would think that Paul VI had somehow conjured up a new teaching out of thin air. In fact, the conjurers were the dissenters who refused to affirm the logical consequences of the vision of marriage set forth by Vatican II.

Chapter Four

Unpopular Truth No. 4: Proclaiming the All-Male Priesthood

If, as the adage goes, every crisis is an opportunity, then faithful Catholics in a time of scandal have a tremendous opportunity to speak out on behalf of preserving the all-male priesthood. While we have discussed so far gender questions dealing with sexual behavior, we are now faced with another type of gender issue. When the question of priestly ordination of women is raised in western countries, there is a natural tendency for defenders of the all-male priesthood to adopt a tone anxious to avoid offending feminist sentiments. Yet, the Church's reasoning and reflections on the necessity of the all-male priesthood are in no way offensive to the dignity of women.

Instead, serious reflection on the basis of the Church's stance will lead to a deeper appreciation of the common vocation of service of all Christians, male and female, and especially to a greater appreciation of the gift of the Eucharist and of the rest of the deposit of faith.

In fact, the question of the all-male priesthood illustrates the large chasm between two very different worlds, the world of historic apostolic faith and the world of modern western secularism. The all-male priesthood is worth defending because it derives from and illuminates that historic apostolic faith.

And that defense is needed. There are organizations, and even websites, dedicated solely to disseminating information to discredit the Church's teaching on the priesthood. Many academic theologians support such efforts. The media highlights poll data, whether accurate or not, saying most American Catholics favor ordaining women. As Avery Cardinal Dulles noted in a speech to American bishops in 1996, voices are needed to affirm the all-male priesthood. He explicitly compared the situation to the outbreak of dissent over *Humanae Vitae* in 1968: "On the one hand you have a pope, backed by the hierarchical leadership of the church, issuing prohibitions with a claim to divine authority and on the other hand a progressivist wing that seeks to correct what it regards as an obsolete, distorted, culture-bound tradition."[51]

Dulles urged the assembled bishops to warn the faithful of efforts to mislead them by groups favoring women's ordination and to undertake an active educational effort to "support the present teaching and clarify the intrinsic connections between gender and priestly ordination" to counteract studies sponsored by those hostile to the Church's teaching.[52] It is time for Catholics to become more informed of the basis for limiting the priesthood to men so they can speak out without inhibition in defense of a key teaching of the Church that is not in the least anti-woman.

As stated by Pope John Paul II in his 1994 declaration *On Reserving Priestly Ordination to Men Alone* (*Ordinatio Sacerdotalis*), this teaching reflects "the constant and universal Tradition of the Church" and "pertains to the Church's divine constitution itself."[53] It should be no surprise that such a teaching is deeply tied to the core of Christian faith.

By looking at statements and commentaries from the Vatican and various theologians, we can enjoy a fuller vision of why this teaching is worth defending without hesitation or anxiety, even in the face of overwhelming cultural correctness. In the end, a fuller vision of the necessity of the all-male priesthood leads us back to that first Eucharist presided over by Jesus at the Last Supper.

This confident approach to speaking about the all-male priesthood is a far cry from defensive protestations that no unjust discrimination is intended. It focuses on the immense value of the all-male priesthood as part of the deposit of faith.

In the Vatican's 1976 *Declaration Regarding the Question of the Admission of Women to Ministerial Priesthood* (in Latin *Inter Insigniores*), the significance of all sacramental signs, including the Catholic priesthood bestowed by holy orders, lies in linking "the person of every period to the supreme event of the history of salvation, in order to enable that person to understand, through all the Bible's wealth of pedagogy and symbolism, what grace they signify and produce."[54] On this basis, we can forcefully present the all-male priesthood as an invaluable sacramental sign of the supreme event of salvation history: Jesus, the incarnation of God as a human being, was a real male born over two thousand years ago.

The same 1976 Vatican declaration emphasizes how the priest, as stated by the third century father St. Cyprian " 'acts in the place of Christ.'"[55] The declaration focuses on the Eucharist where "the priest, who alone has the power to perform it, then acts not only through the effective power conferred on him by Christ, but *in persona Christi* [in the person of Christ], taking the role of Christ, to the point of being his very image, when he pronounces the words of consecration."[56]

The declaration goes on to say that the gender of the priest represents the historical Jesus of Nazareth who presided over the Last Supper for "Christ himself was and remains a man [using the Latin word *vir* meaning male]."[57] That role as image of Christ is why some refer to this theological theme as the iconic argument in which the priest is an icon of Christ.

Witnessing to the maleness of Jesus is important because the fact that "the incarnation of the word took place according to the male sex . . . cannot be disassociated from the economy of salvation: it is indeed, in harmony with the entirety of God's plan as God himself has revealed it, and of which the mystery of the covenant is the nucleus."[58] Thus the priesthood must testify to the maleness of Jesus both as a question of historic fact and as an expression of the mystery of God's covenant with his people.

In an official theological commentary to the 1976 declaration, this historical and incarnational argument is made even more explicit: "[T]he sacraments and the Church herself are closely tied to history, since Christianity is the result of an event: the coming of the Son of God into time and to a country, and his death on the cross under Pontius Pilate outside the walls of Jerusalem. The sacraments are a memorial of saving events. For this reason their signs are linked to those very events."[59] Abolishing the all-male priesthood severs the link to the incarnation of God in the male Jesus.

This Christian historical sense is like a sword that divides thinkers into two camps. The world of the camp that rejects the Christian, and I may add Jewish, historical sense is reflected in the comments of one of America's most prominent literary critics, Harold Bloom. In his bold tour de force on the literary geniuses of Western civilization, Bloom honestly states his rejection of the Judeo-Christian sense of history and proclaims himself a Gnostic who is freed "from theology, from historicizing, and from divinity that is totally distinct from what is most imaginative in the self."[60]

Large sectors of Western academia and popular opinion, consciously or unconsciously, similarly reject the very notion that God acts in particular historical events. Yet, from the very beginning, the distinctive scandal of Christianity has been that God was born as a male infant in a highly obscure setting. Human pride cannot accept the historical facts of the Incarnation as suitable to its spiritual pretensions.

The all-male priesthood also manifests God's covenant as the nuptial mystery in which "for God the chosen people is seen as his ardently loved spouse."[61] The New Testament further develops the idea of the covenant as nuptial mystery originating in the Old Testament so that now "Christ is the bridegroom; the Church is his bride, whom he loves because he has gained her by his blood and made her glorious, holy and without blemish, and henceforth he is inseparable from her."[62] Here is the scriptural and symbolic richness of the male priesthood as an expression of the mystery of salvation.

Abandoning the image of the bridegroom and the bride entails doing violence to both the Old and New Testaments. Interestingly, when, as seen in a prior chapter, John Paul II speaks in his theology of the body about the "nuptial meaning of the body," we also see him making use of the same bridegroom-bride imagery rooted in the New Testament image of Christ and the Church (see his comments on Ephesians 5:21-33 in the work *Theology of the Body* referenced in the bibliography).

Consequently, to admit women to priestly ordination violates the historical and symbolic testimony of the male priest to the facts of the Incarnation and to the depiction of the covenant as the marriage of Christ the bridegroom to His bride, the Church. In addition, the admission of women revises the role of the feminine already set forth by revelation. In the mystery of the Incarnation, God becomes human as a male born of a woman. The feminine is already present and inextricably bound to the Incarnation.

The expression of the role of woman in the Incarnation is, of course, found in Mary, the Mother of God. As aptly stated by another commentator on the 1976 Vatican declaration, the "principle of the 'eternal feminine' in Christianity did not clothe itself in myths, but became history in the Mary-Christ pair."[63] The mystery of the Incarnation already includes woman at its core—and without any physical male contribution to Jesus' conception at that. Changing the image of the bridegroom is not necessary to express the role of the feminine in salvation. The feminine already entered the mystery of the Incarnation when the woman Mary consented to make it possible.

As noted before, in 1994, John Paul II explicitly reaffirmed the teaching of Paul VI and declared an end to debate on this issue. Shortly thereafter, prominent American theologian and now cardinal Avery Dulles evaluated the basis for both popes' teaching and came out in favor of its infallibility:

> I conclude therefore that the Pope and the Congregation for the Doctrine of the
> Faith seem to be on good ground in holding that the Church has no power to
> ordain women to the priesthood. The constancy of the tradition, based as it is

on the practice of Jesus and the teaching of Scripture, supports the idea of infallibility. The Pope and the congregation appear to have a keener sense of the tradition and of the sacramental symbolism than do their critics. Their judgment that the doctrine is indeed infallible deserves to be received with respectful and firm assent.[64]

Although, as Dulles points out, the 1994 apostolic letter *Ordinatio Sacerdotalis* "relies only on arguments from authority," both Dulles and the apostolic letter mention the value of theological arguments in favor of the teaching.[65] The major theological theme supporting such arguments is the same one explained at length in Paul VI's 1976 declaration, namely, that the priest in the Eucharist "acts in the person of Christ the Bridegroom."[66] Dulles terms this the "iconic" argument."[67]

As I have outlined above, this "iconic" argument can be expressed in two ways. The first way emphasizes the historical witness to the Incarnation. The male priest preserves the apostolic witness to the incarnation of God in the male Jesus who instituted the Eucharist at the Last Supper. The second way expresses the nature of the covenant as nuptial mystery with Christ as the bridegroom and the Church as the bride.

In my opinion, the first way, by its emphasizing the facts of the historical Incarnation, is of great value in presenting the importance of the teaching as forcefully as possible in the current cultural climate. For a long time, and especially today, there has been an incessant onslaught on the fundamental doctrines of Christianity as held not only by Catholics and Eastern Orthodox but also as held by Protestant evangelicals. The prime target of that assault has been the chief teaching of Christianity: God became flesh in Jesus.

Thus, the argument that the male priest testifies to the historic male Jesus as the unique incarnation of God should be appealing to those traditional Christians whose beliefs have been under incessant assault. Even Protestant evangelicals who reject any ministerial priesthood and the real presence in the Eucharist can see the value in preserving the all-male minister of the Lord's Supper as an ancient testimony that it was indeed in this male Jesus that God came into the world, no matter how incongruous this may sound to modern religious relativists.

For such relativists, to even speak of a unique incarnation of God is viewed as an act of presumption that denigrates other religious traditions. For many other modern secularists and theological liberals, the notion of a divine incarnation is itself viewed as mere mythology. For such, it is preposterous that mere mythology should keep women from full participation in all roles in the Church.

As a result, the teaching in favor of the all-male priesthood can have a strong ecumenical role among Christians who are keen to defend the traditional core of Christianity. The fact that women's ordination is but one part of a wider agenda by theological liberals and radical feminists should put all traditional Christians on alert when the all-male priesthood is attacked. Reserving ordination to men alone is not a mere policy or personnel matter. As we have seen, changing this teaching does violence to historic Christianity, to the Eucharist, and to the rich scriptural development of the idea of the covenant between God and the people of God.

Once the genuine significance of the Church's teaching on ordination is grasped, it is much more likely that Catholics will be willing to stand up to the political and cultural correctness that seeks to remake the Church in the image of just another organization or association. They may even challenge the survey questions of the media.

The need to be prepared against the secular onslaught on the Church is urgent given the revelations of scandal in the American priesthood. The climate of scandal makes it necessary for all Catholics to be aware that discussions of married clergy and female clergy are not on the same theological and biblical level. It is undisputed that mandatory celibacy is a practice that the Church may conceivably change in the future without doing violence to the sacrament of Holy Orders or to the Eucharist. This point can be acknowledged even by those opposing a married clergy.

On the other hand, women's ordination is a practice that the Church has no authority to ever introduce. The average Catholic probably has no idea of this fundamental difference between the two proposals that are often blithely paired in any media discussion of possible change in the Church. The media does not help matters by treating the issue as equivalent to the question of whether women should be police officers or firefighters.

As urged by Dulles, the situation calls for a strong pastoral effort such as the publications issued by American bishops to explain the basis of this teaching. Yet, as in so many other matters, such as abortion and contraception, many American clerics appear wary of challenging the cultural beliefs of their American parishioners. A marked departure from such pastoral timidity is the only hope for forming Catholics who will not rely on the secular or dissident press or survey questions for their theology.

Complicating the pastoral problem is the widespread presence of heterodox Catholic commentators in the media whose views are inevitably presented as having the same weight as the teachings of the hierarchy. As this situation remains unchallenged, a de facto alternative teaching authority embracing error grows in its power to obscure Catholic truth and mislead both Catholics and non-Catholics alike.

As a result, it is important for Catholics faithful to the genuine magisterium or teaching authority of the Church to be able to speak cogently about this issue. I recall years ago the reaction of high school Catholics when an archbishop defending the Church's doctrine on ordination simply told them that the all-male priesthood was based on tradition. While the archbishop was correct, the students did not seem overly impressed; they were not challenged with specific theological arguments or themes for reflection. In my opinion, no lasting impact was made.

In contrast, from the sources discussed above and other writings, we can formulate at least six "deeper" theological responses to the modern question of admitting women to the priesthood. I classify these six responses or themes as follows: the tradition, the sacramental matter of ordination, the Marian dimension, the nuptial mystery, the eucharistic argument, and the incarnational argument.

The argument from tradition or authority is the basis used by John Paul II to issue his 1994 declaration ending open debate on the issue in the Church and replacing such open debate with education on the basis of the Church's teaching. The Pope's 1994 language and subsequent statements by the Congregation for the Doctrine of the Faith affirm that limiting the priesthood to men is an infallible teaching of the ordinary magisterium or teaching authority of the Church.

As explained in the *Encyclopedia of Catholic Doctrine,* the extraordinary magisterium is exercised when the Pope or a council makes a "solemn proclamation of dogma."[68] The same encyclopedia also notes that the ordinary magisterium includes the other instances of Church teaching, which can in certain circumstances also be infallible.[69] It also states the conditions for infallible teaching by the ordinary magisterium as follows: "that the bishops be in communion with one another and the Pope; that they teach authoritatively on a matter of faith or morals; that they agree in one judgment; and that they propose this as something to be held definitively."[70] The best support for the infallible nature of the teaching on the priesthood is the universal and constant testimony of the tradition throughout the history of the Church, both East and West.

The second theological theme is the argument from sacramental matter. Each of the seven sacraments can be said to consist of form and matter. As one writer puts it, form refers to "the words spoken"; matter refers to "what is seen and felt."[71] In Baptism, the matter is water, and the form consists of the invocation of the Trinity. In the Eucharist, the form lies in the words of consecration, and the matter consists of bread and wine.

Likewise, in Holy Orders, we can say that the matter for ordination is a baptized male candidate and the laying on of hands by the bishop, and that the form refers to the prayer of the bishop in ordaining the candidate. The Church teaches that Christ himself instituted the form and matter of each sacrament, and thus that the Church has no authority to change what Christ has instituted. Just as the Church cannot replace the water of baptism with oil or the eucharistic elements of bread and wine with some other food or beverage, the Church cannot replace Christ's choice of males only for the ministerial priesthood.

The third theme is the Marian theme. John Paul II has explicitly taught that the Church has both a Marian profile and a Petrine profile as developed in the work of Swiss theologian Hans Urs von Balthasar (1905-1988). American theologian George Weigel has drawn attention to the Pope's teaching concerning these two complementary profiles of the Church.

The Marian profile is the Church as discipleship since the Virgin Mary was the first disciple. Weigel explains the comparison of the Marian and the Petrine profiles: "The 'Marian profile,' John Paul said, is even 'more . . . fundamental' in Catholicism than the 'Petrine profile.' Though the two cannot be divided, the 'Marian Church,' the Church formed in the image of a woman and her discipleship, precedes, makes possible, and indeed makes sense of the 'Petrine Church,' the Church of office and authority formed in the image of Peter."[72]

Limiting the ministerial priesthood to males can be viewed as part of the Petrine dimension of the Church. But more fundamental is the calling to the common priesthood of the faithful of all Catholics, male and female, as disciples through the sacraments of Baptism and Confirmation: the Marian dimension of the Church. These ideas present the truth of the complementary roles of the ministerial and common priesthoods in the Church, as opposed to the erroneous view of the ministerial priesthood as the sole vehicle for a full Christian vocation.

A fourth theme in affirming the papal teaching on the priesthood is the nuptial mystery. As noted before, this theme of God as the bridegroom and the chosen people as the bride begins in the Old Testament prophets and reaches its full development in the Pauline epistles where Jesus is presented as the bridegroom and the Church as the bride. This mystery, which touches on a wide range of topics such as God's covenant, the new chosen people, the sacramentality of marriage, and the second coming of Christ, is a rich scriptural expression of salvation. The male priesthood is a tangible expression of that deeply rooted teaching.

In treating of the ordination issue, most writings appropriately focus on the sacrament of Holy Orders. Yet, it is impossible to separate any focus on the priesthood from the Eucharist. The eucharistic argument in support of denying ordination to women is that the male priest acts in the person of Christ in consecrating the bread and the wine in direct continuity with Christ at the Last Supper. From this perspective, the maleness of the priest is not only necessary to express the nuptial mystery but also to express the full historical meaning of the Eucharist as a re-presentation of Christ presiding over the Last Supper.

This eucharistic argument has a paschal dimension as well. It is fitting for the male priest to stand for the male Christ who in turn is the male paschal or Passover lamb required by the Old Testament.

Finally, I submit that the argument that has the ecumenical potential of appealing to all traditional Christians, whether they hold the Catholic and Orthodox view of a sacramental priesthood or, like evangelical Protestants, view ministry as non-sacramental, is the argument that the male priest testifies to the historical fact that God chose to become incarnate as a male. As stated earlier, the value of this incarnational argument is readily apparent in the current climate of radical deconstruction of traditional Christian beliefs in which the divinity of Christ and even the concept of a deity itself are put in question by persons still boldly claiming to be Christian theologians. In this context, even evangelical Protestants will be able to see the value of the consistent Catholic and Orthodox witness to a male priesthood that witnesses to the basic facts of the Incarnation.

The attacks on fundamental Christian belief are even more severe from the perspective of radical feminist theology which seeks, as theologian Rosemary Ruether has stated, "a WomanChrist."[73] The male priesthood is a bulwark against such strange historical revisionism.

The six theological themes outlined above put some flesh on what for many Catholics remains a little explained but fundamental teaching of the Church. If, as John Paul II has declared, reserving the priesthood to men alone is a matter "which pertains to the Church's divine constitution itself" and which "is to be definitively held by all the Church's faithful," then we should all be prepared to speak confidently in favor of this teaching.[74] And, certainly, this teaching, once understood more deeply as coherently embedded in Christian revelation, should pose no obstacle for non-Catholics inquiring about the Church.

Chapter Five

Unpopular Truth No. 5: Peter Was the First Bishop of Rome

The question of whether Peter was indeed the first bishop of Rome has recently gained popular prominence due to the American best seller by historian and papal critic Garry Wills who vigorously dismisses the entire idea as myth. Although simplistically and sensationally presented, Wills' thesis relies on the view of other, albeit more subtle, critical scholars that Peter could not have been a bishop at Rome allegedly because there were no bishops in Rome until the middle of the second century A.D. To treat this issue will entail a more technical presentation than in the previous essays. But given the distortions presented in the popular press, this detailed analysis is necessary.

Several years ago, David Albert Jones, O.P., challenged in the British journal *New Blackfriars* the common view that there were no bishops in the first century.[75] One scholar, Francis

Sullivan, S.J., recently responded specifically to Jones' challenge. Sullivan reaffirmed the apparent majority view that there were no bishops in the first century.[76]

This chapter will briefly refer to Sullivan's critique of Jones, and will present in a new light the New Testament evidence showing that Jones' challenge of the reigning critical view that there were no bishops in the first century is indeed well-founded and long overdue. That Peter was the first bishop of Rome is an unpopular Catholic truth, unpopular, as we have seen, even with some so-called Catholics. It is too important a truth to leave to specialized journals or to Garry Wills. This chapter requires some close reading and reasoning, but for that I will not apologize. Others have unnecessarily created the smoke that needs to be cleared.

The heart of Jones' challenge to those denying Peter's episcopacy in Rome is to highlight the flawed assumptions underlying the reasoning used to deny a first century episcopate: 1.) the ideological tendency to view apostolic ministry as "free, loose, inspired and lay" while seeing "the emergence of clerical forms as a fall from primitive innocence" (Jones, p. 142); and 2.) the denial of the existence of a first century episcopate based on the alleged silence of early documents.

In essence, Jones rightly detects a pervasive bias in the critical literature against developed church structure as somehow contaminating the springtime of apostolic Christianity. As a result, many critical scholars refuse to recognize the New Testament evidence for the early episcopate. This bias fits well the emphasis in some contemporary theological circles on democratizing the Church under the rubric of "collegiality." But, of course, as Jones points out, this bias against church structure first arose as part of the old Protestant idea that the biblical church was fatally corrupted by later structural developments in Catholicism.

The mindset identified by Jones becomes most apparent in the critical literature's consistently limiting the term "bishop" to a quite narrow and anachronistic definition. Explicitly or implicitly, the scholars denying a first century episcopate will usually define "bishop" as denoting "a solitary permanent resident church administrator for one city."

On its face, this definition is quite narrow and rigid. In fact, it is anachronistic in the sense of projecting back into the first century a definition that is so narrow that it results in the a priori exclusion from serious consideration of most of the uses of the Greek word *episkopos* or bishop. *Episkopos* is the Greek word meaning "overseer" that has been traditionally translated as "bishop." This word is found in the first century documents at issue, namely, the New Testament and Clement's First Letter to the Corinthians (I Clement) written from Rome circa 95 A.D.

In the course of this chapter, we will take a close look at this particular Greek word in its various forms as used in the New Testament, which, of course, has come down to us in Greek manuscripts.

To Sullivan's credit as a scholar, he explicitly defines, unlike some others, his narrow description of a bishop: "A 'bishop' is a residential pastor who presides in a stable manner over the church in a city and its environs" (Sullivan, p. 14). What Sullivan left out, but assumes throughout his book, is that the title bishop can apply to only *one* such residential pastor per city. What this arbitrary definition, promulgated without discussion, does is to automatically exclude any apostle as a bishop because the apostles, especially Peter and Paul, were primarily missionaries moving from place to place founding new churches. Thus, by means of a rigid and arbitrary definition, the debate about first century bishops is fatally skewed from the beginning toward upholding the thesis that there were no first century bishops.

Moreover, when a first century document fails to speak explicitly of bishops in this particular narrow sense, the document is said to be "silent" about the episcopacy. And this alleged "silence" is then interpreted as proving the nonexistence of a first century episcopate.

Ironically, after foisting this anachronistic definition on the debate, these same scholars will in turn label any attempt to call an apostle a "bishop"— not surprisingly— anachronistic! The end result is that any attempt to go back to the first century texts themselves to see how they define a bishop is rejected because the definition has already been predetermined.

Thus, the first step in viewing the entire matter in a new light is to undo the hijacking of the term "bishop" by letting the first century texts themselves define a first century bishop and to see if this new definition would include an apostle like Peter. If so, then there is no plausible basis to deny Peter's status as the first or founding bishop of Rome.

Jones begins this effort to return to the texts by noting that "of the five New Testament occurrences of *episkopos* in the sense of an office holder, three are in the singular. . . ."(Jones, p. 131). Jones makes this point as a way of demonstrating that there was such a thing as a "mono-episcopate" in the first century. What we mean by "mono-episcopate" is that there were single individuals recognized as the preeminent bishops of a particular city or region, not merely an undifferentiated council of church leaders. In response to Jones' view favoring single bishops, Sullivan demurs and says that he can find only two such instances of *episkopos* in the singular: I Timothy 3:2 and Titus 1:7 (Sullivan, p. 219).

Unfortunately, Jones limited his reference to singular occurrences of *episkopos* used "in the sense of an office holder," which allows Sullivan to exclude the singular reference to Christ as bishop in 1 Peter 2:25. This exclusion of the reference to Christ as bishop is unwarranted. The highly significant use of *episkopos* in reference to Christ cannot but tell us something important about what "bishop" meant to first century Christians when applied to their fellow Christians.

In any event, Jones' argument is more precise: the use of the singular allows us to infer "mono-episcopacy," defined as referring to "the chief presbyter overseeing the local church" (Jones, p. 132). It is worth noting that Jones does not argue that only the chief presbyter was called bishop in the first century, but rather that mono-episcopacy "is one possible use of the term even then, and one that would later become standard" (Jones, p. 132).

In effect, Jones and I are saying that the chief presbyter filled the role of a single bishop in a particular town or city. Presbyter is the term for "elder" in the New Testament which is derived from the Greek word *presbuteros* or *presbyteros.*

While I agree with Jones' quite reasonable and path-breaking argument, my own approach is broader. Why not look at all five occurrences of *episkopos,* whether singular or plural, to derive a first century definition of bishop? Sullivan and other scholars place much emphasis on whether references to church offices in the New Testament are in the singular or the plural as indicating the stark alternatives of either collegial or one-man rule. I submit that it is more logical to focus instead on first defining what bishop meant in the first century in order to judge later the significance, if any, of using the plural or the singular in a particular context. It may be that a genuinely first century definition does not necessarily pose the stark alternatives assumed by many scholars.

As stated by Jones and documented by the late biblical scholar Raymond Brown, there are five occurrences of *episkopos* referring to a "'supervisor, overseer, superintendent, [or] bishop'" in the New Testament: Acts 20:28 (in the plural); Philippians 1:1 (plural); 1 Timothy 3:2 (singular); Titus 1:7 (singular); 1 Peter 2:25 (singular).[77] But this short list is incomplete for our purposes.

The related word *episkope* referring to the office or position of a supervisor or bishop is also found in 1 Timothy 3:1 in connection with the use of *episkopos* in 1 Timothy 3:2 (Brown, p. 323). *Episkope* is also found in Acts 1:20, Luke 19:44, and 1 Peter 2:12.

In addition, biblical scholar Raymond Brown documents the verb form *episkopein* meaning "'to supervise, oversee, inspect, care for'" as occurring in 1 Peter 5:2 and Hebrews 12:15 (Brown, p. 323).

The challenge is to compose a first century definition of a bishop, his office, and his function by considering all of these occurrences. This approach is quite different from the hyperanalytical method of much scholarly discussion. In other words, we are trying to construct a synthetic definition, not deconstruct the text into unrelated pieces. All of these Greek words are related and should be considered together in our search for a reasonable definition of "bishop."

Yet, there is even more to consider because any discussion of a bishop implicates discussion of pastor or shepherd. Thus, New Testament references to church leaders as shepherds must also be taken into account in order to understand first century references to bishops, especially when considering the role of Peter (John 21:15-17) (Brown, p. 325).

Moreover, the term presbyter cannot be ignored since many scholars agree and, most importantly, the texts themselves (including several texts listed above plus 1 Timothy 5:17) indicate a tendency to use presbyter and bishop interchangeably (Brown, p. 333). As noted before, presbyter is the English form of the Greek *presbuteros* that means "elder." It is the root for our English word "priest" and is still used today by Catholics to refer to members of the priesthood. Thus, there is a wealth of New Testament passages to consider in formulating a definition of bishop in the first century.

Any a priori attempt to limit the scope of the texts to be considered should be resisted, including attempts based on whether the word is singular or plural, or on whether the word is being used to refer to a person in contrast to an office, or is being used as a verb. Only by avoiding such arbitrary limits can we be faithful to the texts themselves as opposed to following mere convention.

If we consider Acts 1:20, we see Peter explaining that a replacement for Judas Iscariot is needed. Peter quotes the Psalms stating: "His office let another take." (Unless stated otherwise, all scriptural references are to the Revised Standard Version or RSV.) The word translated as "office" is *episkope* referring to the office of bishop. In the Authorized or King James Version, the translation is "his bishopric let another take." *Episkope* is the same word used in 1 Timothy 3:1: "If anyone aspires to the office of bishop, he desires a noble task." I Timothy 3:2

then continues this line of thought by using *episkopos* in the familiar passage: "Now a bishop must be above reproach. . . ."

Thus, in Acts 1:20, Peter ties the office of apostle vacated by Judas to the office of supervisor or bishop. The same word used by Peter in Acts is then used in I Timothy to refer to a local church leader. This convergence contradicts the attempts by some to totally divorce the functions of an apostle from that of a bishop. The sensible inference is that the office of apostle includes the function of a bishop. Once this perspective is adopted, the idea that Peter could not possibly have been a bishop in Rome becomes implausible. It is appropriate to compare the use of these terms in Acts and in the Pastoral Epistles because both sets of documents appear to have originated at the end of the first century.[78]

Is it legitimate to make this synthetic connection? Yes, because we have the same Greek word, a similar context, and roughly the same historical point in time.

Furthermore, in 1 Peter 5:1, Peter refers to himself as a "fellow elder" or presbyter. Even if, as some speculate, Peter did not write this epistle himself, we have at the minimum a hypothetical first century disciple of Peter calling Peter a presbyter, probably in the time period 70 to 90 A.D. (Brown Intro., p. 706).

As stated before, critical scholars customarily point out how *episkopos* and presbyter are used interchangeably in the New Testament. This usage is also apparent in 1 Peter. In the next verse, 1 Peter 5:2, the presbyters or elders are exhorted to "tend the flock of God." The RSV notes that some ancient authorities add *episkopein* to this verse to signify "exercising the oversight." Given the reference to both elders and the exercise of oversight in this passage, Peter is in effect identified by himself, or at least by a close disciple, as a presbyter-bishop.

Even if we ignore the disputed presence of *episkopein* added by only some ancient authorities, it remains true that presbyter and *episkopos* appear to be used interchangeably at other points in the New Testament and in I Clement. This usage in 1 Peter makes it difficult to accept the thesis that Peter would not have been considered a bishop or *episkopos* while resident in Rome.

Further reinforcement for this conclusion comes from the use of *episkopein* in Hebrews 12:15 urging Christians to "[s]ee to it [*episkopountes*] that no one fail to obtain the grace of God; that no 'root of bitterness' spring up and cause trouble, and by it the many become defiled." Although a general charge to all Christians, it is a charge especially suitable to the mission of bishops to maintain "sound doctrine" and "to confute those who contradict it," as described in Titus 1:7-15. It is a role that Peter dramatically carried out in Acts 5:1-6, in "striking down unworthy members of the community" (Brown, p. 325). Again, all of these documents under consideration appear to date from the latter part of the first century.

Also in 1 Peter is the reference to Christ as "the Shepherd and Guardian of your souls" (1

Peter 2:25). The word translated in the RSV as "Guardian" is none other than *episkopos*. The Authorized or King James Version is more revealing of the underlying Greek text by consistently translating *episkopos* as bishop. The King James translation, unlike some other translations, thus allows the English reader to see that the same Greek word is appearing again.

This reference to Christ as Bishop is important because critical scholars have a tendency to say that an apostle like Peter could not have been a mere administrator as these scholars say *episkopos* implies. In contrast to this view of the *episkopos* as a mere administrator, here is *episkopos* applied to Christ Himself and thus clearly not limited to a mere functionary or some sort of lower level administrator of church finances or goods.[79] As a result, it becomes even more plausible that Peter the leader of the apostles would have been called *episkopos* in first century Rome.

Calling Christ a bishop is significant, because in John 21:15-17, Christ commissions Peter to feed and tend his sheep. Accordingly, it would be natural to view the same Peter that succeeds Christ as shepherd of the sheep as also succeeding Christ as *episkopos*. This natural connection is unavoidable given that 1 Peter 2:25 calls Christ both Shepherd and Bishop of souls.

In addition, as noted before, in 1 Peter 5:2, some authorities tie the exhortation for elders to shepherd the flock to the idea of exercising oversight (*episkopein*). Thus, there is an undeniable interrelation between the idea of shepherd, elder, and *episkopos.*

Chapter 21 of the Gospel of John where Christ commissions Peter as shepherd is usually dated like 1 Peter to the late first century, although Brown believes that John 21 was "perhaps" added to the gospel in the time period 100 to 110 A.D. (Brown Intro., pp. 374-376). Even under this later and admittedly speculative dating, I submit that 1 Peter and John 21 are close enough in time to merit considering them together.

In addition to using *episkopos* to refer to Christ, *episkope* is translated as referring to God's "visitation" in 1 Peter 2:12. In this instance, *episkope* is used in reference to God himself "visiting" mankind. A similar use is found in Luke 19:44. This use reinforces the conclusion that neither *episkope* nor *episkopos* is limited to lower level administrative tasks unworthy of an apostle like Peter, and again makes it plausible that Roman Christians would not have hesitated to refer to Peter's presence as *episcope* or visitation.

Reliance on 1 Peter to infer Roman usage is particularly appropriate given that 1 Peter is viewed as having been written in Rome itself (Brown Intro., p. 706). It is also noteworthy that Brown considers that "[o]f all the Catholic Epistles, I Peter has the best chance of being written by the figure to whom it is attributed"— that is, Peter himself (Brown Intro., p. 718). If Peter did indeed write 1 Peter, the date of authorship is probably 60 to 63 A.D. (Brown, Intro., p. 706). Prior to this time, we already have the earliest use of *episkopos* in the New Testament in or about 56 A.D. in Philippians 1:1, which, interestingly, also possibly originated in Rome (Brown Intro., p. 484). All of this information makes the notion of Peter as a bishop in Rome historically persuasive.

To summarize, a good first century definition of bishop would be that of a shepherd especially charged to forcefully protect the sound doctrine and peace of the local church. This is a role exercised by Peter, among others, in the New Testament. There is no reason to doubt that Peter exercised the same role while resident in Rome prior to his martyrdom. There is also no reason to doubt that the Roman Christians would have described Peter as *episkopos* in carrying out this function. In fact, a serious argument can be made that the Roman Christians would see the arrival of Peter as a highly significant visitation similar to the visitation of God referred to in Luke and Hebrews.

It is plain common sense that, while in Rome, Peter would not have been just one more *episkopos* among many, but rather the chief or preeminent *episkopos*. It is even tempting to call him "archbishop" solely in the literal Greek sense of the "chief *episkopos*" or *archi-episkopos* (cf. 1 Peter 5:4). The undisputed chief of the apostles who struck down false Christians in Acts would clearly take a preeminently authoritative role in Rome.

Thus, the existence of a group or college of presbyter-bishops does not exclude or minimize the role of Peter as the preeminent bishop. Jones correctly makes this possibility plain: "In a community in which the collegiate overseers were called *episkopoi,* there could still have been the *role* of head bishop, just as the same role existed in churches that used a different vocabulary" (Jones, p. 137). In the case of Peter, such a role is certainly much more than a mere possibility given his apostolic prestige and close connection to the events of the earthly ministry of Jesus.

Given the above, can we fairly add to Peter's role as chief bishop of Rome the notion that he was the first or founding bishop of Rome? While it appears that Roman Christians pre-dated Peter's arrival in Rome,[80] there is no reason to deny early Church tradition that Peter along with Paul laid the foundation, through preaching and martyrdom, for the Church in Rome. To be precise, we can fairly say that Peter was the first or founding chief presbyter-bishop of the Church in Rome.

This scenario raises the question of Paul's role. Even those who would reject the thesis of this article admit that the early church made a distinction between Peter as "chief shepherd" and Paul as a teacher of doctrine.[81] This traditional view plus Peter's preeminent role among the Twelve and his prominence in the events of Jesus' earthly ministry make such a distinction between Peter and Paul credible.

In addition, Paul himself acknowledged the special role of Peter, even in the tension of disagreement, as one who was considered a "pillar" of the church whose approval was highly desirable (see Galatians 2:9 & Brown Intro., p. 707). To my original suggestion that we can call

Peter "*archi-episkopos*" in the sense of "chief bishop," we can now add another possible meaning to "*archi-episkopos*" as meaning "first or beginning bishop" because the Greek prefix *archi* is related to "*arche*" which means "first or beginning." In this linguistic relation between being the "chief" bishop and the "first" bishop, we have a clue as to how Peter as "chief" bishop of Rome would become the recognized "first" bishop of Rome.

In sum, this survey of the New Testament view of the interrelated identities of bishop, shepherd, and elder, and the consideration of Peter's leading role among the apostles yield persuasive evidence that the first century Roman Christians would not have hesitated to view Peter as the founding chief bishop or shepherd of the Roman church. Although denial of this evidence is common, the textual evidence for this conclusion remains persuasive in spite of its unpopularity.

Thus, those who would cast doubt on the Catholic claim that the Pope is the successor of Peter by debunking the notion of Peter as the first bishop of Rome are on quite shaky ground. Their speculations are the product of a contemporary agenda: the undermining of papal authority for a variety of reasons.

Catholics and others should take such speculation debunking the role of Peter as the first bishop of Rome with a grain of salt. There is excellent common sense evidence for saying Peter was the first bishop of Rome. The smoke and mirrors raised by some (I am not referring to responsible and respected scholars like Sullivan) should not stand in the way of those who are attracted by the teachings of John Paul II.

So it is fitting in a collection of essays that in large part presents the evangelizing work of John Paul II that we end by clearing away the confusion sown by those who seek to undermine his work and his authority.

Conclusion

T hese essays have spanned a wide variety of
topics: abortion, chastity, contraception,
the all-male priesthood, and the primacy of Peter in Rome. What unites these themes is that
they are on the cutting edge of unpopularity in
the secular West. The new apologetics of the
New Evangelization should be bold in addressing what is in most need of being addressed
and in refusing to settle for inoffensive platitudes.

In a striking essay, Bishop Allen Vigneron
has written with vision on the role of philosophy in the New Evangelization.[82] He has called
for the New Evangelization to create a "culture
of communion" to evangelize secular modernity
and its emphasis on the self (pp. 102-103). In
this task, the bishop hails John Paul's theology
of the body as a way of advancing the culture of
communion by seeing the body as inherently
predisposed for communion (p. 107).

Vigneron also recommends to those involved in the New Evangelization a "'wide-
mindedness,' a readiness to stretch themselves
beyond the usual boundaries of their intellectual capital" (p. 105). In a small way, this book
of apologetics aims to practice that advice.
From the foreword which borrows insights from

a non-Catholic European philosopher to arguments that address hard-fought issues from a fresh perspective, the intent of this book is to come close to the "wide-mindedness" needed to awaken the energies of a modernity too often given to despair. Like Vigneron, I see the Pope's call for the New Evangelization as a bold strategy, a strategy that calls for new departures so that the springtime of faith can arise in a new millennium. The bishop describes our era as similar to the era of "ferment and creativity" that marked the work of the early Church Fathers who implanted the Gospel in the Hellenistic world (p. 104). May all our voices together be worthy of this moment.

Notes

[1] Ronald Dworkin, *Life's Dominion: An Argument About Abortion, Euthanasia, and Individual Freedom* (N.Y.: Alfred A. Knopf, 1993), p. 164 .

[2] Dworkin, p. 165.

[3] Dr. Bernard Nathanson, *The Hand of God* (Washington, D.C.: Regnery Publishing, 1996), p. 191.

[4] Dworkin, p. 160.

[5] Nathanson, pp. 140-47.

[6] Even Dworkin admits that "electrical brain activity arises in a fetus's brain stem, and it is capable of reflex movement, by approximately the seventh week after conception." Dworkin, p. 17. The famous Silent Scream video hosted by Dr. Nathanson depicts the abortion of a 12-week fetus (child). It is readily accessible on the internet for those who can face it.

[7] Nathanson, Ch. 10, pp. 125-39.

[8] Julie B. Carr, *Countdown to a Miracle: The Making of Me* (n.p.: Motherly Way Enterprises, 1999), p. 252.

[9] Carr, p. 244. *The Merck Manual* (Home Edition 1997), p. 1138, dates this event even earlier at 20 days or about 3 weeks after fertilization.

[10] Carr, p. 232.

[11] Carr, p. 216. *The Merck Manual* (Home Edition 1997), p. 1138, dates this event slightly later at about 10 weeks after fertilization.

[12] John Collins Harvey, M.D., "Distinctly Human: The When, Where, & How of Life's Beginning," *Commonweal* 129, no. 3 (Feb. 8, 2002) (article begins at p. 11). Available from www.commonwealmagazine.org, but with no pagination.

[13] Jan E. Jirasek, M.D., D.Sc., ed., *An Atlas of the Human Embryo and Fetus: A Photographic Review of Human Prenatal Development* (N.Y.: The Parthenon Publishing Group, 2001) (hereinafter "Jirasek"). This book is part of *The Encyclopedia of Visual Medicine Series.*

[14] Louis G. Keith, M.D., foreword to Jirasek, p.7.

[15] Jirasek, Fig. 4.9, p. 76.

[16] Jirasek, Fig. 5.13, p. 93.

[17] Jirasek, Fig. 5.16, p. 95.

[18] Jirasek, Fig. 6.1, p. 97.

[19] Jirasek, Fig. 6.2, p. 98.

[20] Randy Alcorn, *ProLife Answers to ProChoice Arguments* (Sisters, OR: Multnomah Publishers, 2000), p. 65. Dworkin, citing medical texts, agrees with this pro-life source. See Dworkin, p. 17.

[21] *Roe v. Wade,* 410 U.S. 113, 163-64 (1973) (all quotations are from the court reporter's syllabus or summary abstract of the decision). The text of the *Roe* and *Planned Parenthood* decisions, plus that of other relevant court decisions, is conveniently available to lawyer and non-lawyer alike at the Abortion Law Homepage website.

[22] *Roe* at pp. 163-64.

[23] *Roe* at pp. 163-65.

[24] *Planned Parenthood v. Casey,* 505 U.S. at 870.

[25] Edward H. Levi, *An Introduction to Legal Reasoning* (Chicago: University of Chicago Press, 1972), pp. 8-27.

[26] Levi, at p. 103.

[27] *Casey,* at p. 856.

[28] Levi, at p. 59.

[29] *Webster's Ninth New Collegiate Dictionary* (1990), s.v. "meretricious."

[30] *Webster's Ninth New Collegiate Dictionary* (1990), s.v. "meretricious."

[31] John Paul II, *The Theology of the Body: Human Love in the Divine Plan* (Boston: Pauline Books & Media, 1997), p. 45 (hereafter "Body").

[32] Body, p. 45.

[33] Body, p. 47.

[34] Body, p. 61.

[35] Body, p. 62.

[36] Body, p. 63.

[37] Body, p. 63 (quoting Vatican II's *Gaudium et Spes,* article 24).

[38] Body, pp. 64-65 (again borrowing from *Gaudium et Spes,* art. 24).

[39] Body, p. 65.

[40] Body, p. 127.

[41] Body, p. 127.

[42] John Paul II, *Evangelium Vitae* (The Gospel of Life), 13.3, in *The Encyclicals of John Paul II,* ed. J. Michael Miller, C.S.B. (Huntington, Ind.: Our Sunday Visitor, 2001), p. 691 (hereafter "Miller").

[43] Miller, p. 691.

[44] Miller, p. 691.

[45] *Planned Parenthood v. Casey,* 505 U.S. at 857.

[46] *Gaudium et Spes,* 48, in *The Sixteen Documents of Vatican II,* ed. Marianne Lorraine Trouvé, FSP (Boston: Pauline Books & Media 1999), p. 671 (introductions by Douglas G. Bushman, S.T.L.) (hereafter all translations of Vatican II documents will be from this collection).

[47] Karol Wojtyla, *Love and Responsibility,* trans. H.T. Willetts (San Francisco: Ignatius Press, 1993), p. 66.

[48] Wojtyla, p. 41.

[49] Wojtyla, p. 67.

[50] Wojtyla, p. 68.

[51] Avery Dulles, S.J., "Pastoral Response to the Teaching on Women's Ordination," *Origins* 26:11 (Aug. 29, 1996): 178.

[52] Dulles, "Pastoral Response," 180.

[53] John Paul II, *Ordinatio Sacerdotalis* (Boston: Pauline Books & Media, 1994), p. 7.

[54] Congregation for the Doctrine of the Faith, *From "Inter Insigniores" to "Ordinatio Sacerdotalis"* (Washington, D.C.: United States Catholic Conference, 1998), p. 37 (hereafter "CDF").

[55] CDF, p. 41.

[56] CDF, p. 41.

[57] CDF, p. 43.

[58] CDF, p. 43.

[59] CDF, pp. 67-68.

[60] Harold Bloom, *Genius: A Mosaic of One Hundred Exemplary Creative Minds* (N.Y.: Warner Books, 2002), p. xviii (hereafter "Bloom").

[61] CDF, p. 43.

[62] CDF, p. 45.

[63] CDF, pp. 87, 88.

[64] Avery Dulles, S.J., "Tradition says no," *The Tablet* 249:8105 (Dec. 9, 1995): 1573 (hereafter "Dulles").

[65] Dulles, p. 1573.

[66] Dulles, p. 1573.

[67] Dulles, p. 1573.

[68] "Ordinary Magisterium," in *Encyclopedia of Catholic Doctrine*, ed. Russell Shaw (Huntington, Ind.: Our Sunday Visitor Publishing, 1997), p. 481(hereafter "Shaw").

[69] Shaw, p. 481.

[70] Shaw, p. 481.

[71] Christopher M. Buckner, "Sacrament," in *Encyclopedia of Catholic Doctrine*, ed. Russell Shaw, p. 588 (see n. 64).

[72] George Weigel, *The Truth of Catholicism: Ten Controversies Explored* (N.Y.: Harper Collins, 2001), p. 46.

[73] Rosemary Radford Ruether, *Womanguides: Readings Toward a Feminist Theology* (Boston: Beacon Press, 1985), p. 113.

[74] John Paul II, *Ordinatio Sacerdotalis*, 7.

[75] David Albert Jones, O.P., "Was there a bishop of Rome in the first century?" *New Blackfriars* 80, no. 937 (March 1999): 128 (hereafter "Jones").

[76] Francis A. Sullivan, S.J., *From Apostles to Bishops: The Development of the Episcopacy in the Early Church* (N.Y.: Newman Press, 2001), pp. 219-221 (hereafter "Sullivan").

[77] Raymond E. Brown, S.S., "*Episkope* and *Episkopos:* The New Testament Evidence," *Theological Studies* 41 (1980): 323 (hereafter "Brown").

[78] Raymond E. Brown, S.S., *An Introduction to the New Testament* (N.Y.: Doubleday, 1997), pp. 280, 668 (hereafter "Brown Intro.").

[79] *The Epistle of St. Ignatius of Antioch to the Romans* (ch. 9:1), dating from 98 to 117 A.D., also refers to Christ as overseer or bishop. See Cyril C. Richardson, ed., *Early Christian Fathers* (N.Y.: Simon & Schuster, 1996 ed.), p. 106 & n. 80.

[80] J.M.R. Tillard, O.P., *The Bishop of Rome* (Wilmington, Del.: Michael Glazier, Inc., 1983), p. 83.

[81] Garry Wills, *Why I am a Catholic* (N.Y.: Houghton Mifflin, 2002), pp. 75-76.

[82] Bishop Allen Vigneron, "The New Evangelization and the Teaching of Philosophy," in *The Two Wings of Catholic Thought: Essays on Fides et ratio,* ed. David Foster & Joseph Koterski, S.J. (Washington, D.C.: Catholic University of America Press, 2003), pp. 99-108.

Bibliography

(The works below include sources cited in the endnotes plus other sources that have served as background reading material for the author. Cited sources are listed in the order discussed in the text.)

Foreword
Ortega y Gasset, José. *Man and Crisis.* New York: W.W. Norton & Co., 1958.

_____. *Man and People.* New York: W.W. Norton & Co., 1963.

_____. *The Origin of Philosophy.* New York: W.W. Norton & Co., 1967.

_____. *The Revolt of the Masses.* New York: W.W. Norton & Co., 1994.

_____. *Some Lessons in Metaphysics.* New York: W.W. Norton & Co., 1976.

Some Spanish works about and by Ortega follow: Garagorri, Paulino. *Introducción a Ortega.* Madrid: Alianza Editorial, 1970.

Ortega y Gasset, José. *Meditación de la Técnica y Otros Ensayos Sobre Ciencia y Filosofia.* Madrid: Alianza Editorial, 1982.

(It should be noted that Ortega did not identify himself as a Catholic.)

In the *Catechism of the Catholic Church* (hereafter "*Catechism*"), the following sections dealing with the mass media, journalists, and government control of opinion warn us of the dangers of mass thinking in society: 2496-2499. Section 1779 calling us to self-examination in order to form our consciences is especially appropriate in an age of mass manipulation.

Chapter One: Abortion

Dworkin, Ronald. *Life's Dominion: An Argument About Abortion, Euthanasia, and Individual Freedom. N.Y.:* Alfred A. Knopf, 1993.

Nathanson, Dr. Bernard. *The Hand of God.* Washington, D.C.: Regnery Publishing, 1996.

Carr, Julie B., *Countdown to a Miracle: The Making of Me. N.p.:* Motherly Way Enterprises, 1999.

The Merck Manual. N.Y.: Simon & Schuster 1997 (Home Edition).

Harvey, M.D., John Collins. "Distinctly Human: The When, Where, & How of Life's Beginning." *Commonweal,* Vol. 129, No. 3 (Feb. 8, 2002):11ff. Available from www.commonwealmagazine.org.

Jirasek, M.D., D.Sc., Jan E., ed. *An Atlas of the Human Embryo and Fetus: A Photographic Review of Human Prenatal Development. N.Y.:* The Parthenon Publishing Group, 2001 (foreword by Louis G. Keith, M.D.). This book is part of *The Encyclopedia of Visual Medicine Series.*

Alcorn, Randy. *ProLife Answers to ProChoice Arguments.* Sisters, OR: Multnomah Publishers 2000.

Roe v. Wade, 410 U.S. 113, 163-64 (1973). The text of the *Roe* decision, plus that of other rele-

vant modern court decisions, is conveniently
available to lawyer and non-lawyer alike at the
Abortion Law Homepage website (you can use
the words "Abortion Law Homepage" to search
for the site in Google).
Planned Parenthood v. Casey, 505 U.S. 833
(1992).
Levi, Edward H. An Introduction to Legal Reasoning. Chicago: University of Chicago
Press, 1972.
In the Catechism, section 2273 on abortion is
eloquent in emphasizing that the issue of abortion is a civil rights issue for society, not an issue of imposing a sectarian religious view on
everyone in society.

Chapter Two: Chastity as Integrity

John Paul II. *The Theology of the Body: Human
Love in the Divine Plan.* Boston: Pauline
Books & Media, 1997.
Karol Wojtyla. *Love and Responsibility.* Translated by H.T. Willetts. San Francisco: Ignatius
Press, 1993.
The *Catechism* at sections 2338 through 2345
treats of chastity under the heading "The
integrity of the person." See especially sections
2338 and 2344 for the doctrinal foundations of
my own analysis. For those who seek the integrity of chastity, the perennial question, so dramatically and still relevantly portrayed by St.
Augustine in his *Confessions,* is how. Section
1832 lists the traditional fruits of the Holy
Spirit, among which is chastity. The specifically
Christian way of chastity is through the power

of the Holy Spirit with the body as the temple of the Holy Spirit. While certainly non-believers can be chaste, the Christian tradition realistically recognizes that God must be intimately involved in this quest for integrity.

Chapter Three: Open to Life

John Paul II. *Evangelium Vitae* (The Gospel of Life). In *The Encyclicals of John Paul II,* edited by J. Michael Miller, C.S.B., 681-762. Huntington, Ind.: Our Sunday Visitor, 2001.

Second Vatican Council. *Gaudium et Spes* (Pastoral Constitution on the Church in the Modern World). In *The Sixteen Documents of Vatican II,* edited by Marianne Lorraine Trouvé, FSP, 627-719. Boston: Pauline Books & Media, 1999 (introductions by Douglas Bushman, S.T.L.).

Karol Wojtyla. *Love and Responsibility.* Translated by H.T. Willetts. San Francisco: Ignatius Press, 1993.

The best single source in my experience for the Catholic teaching on contraception is Janet Smith's *Why Humanae Vitae Was Right: A Reader* (San Francisco: Ignatius Press 1993). The book includes an appendix with Prof. Smith's own translation of Paul VI's encyclical *Humanae Vitae* from the official Latin text. The *Catechism* proclaims the teaching that the marital act must be open to life in sections 2366 to 2372.

Chapter Four: The All-Male Priesthood

Dulles, S.J., Avery. "Pastoral Response to the Teaching on Women's Ordination." *Origins* 26:11 (Aug. 29, 1996).

John Paul II, *Ordinatio Sacerdotalis.* Boston: Pauline Books & Media, 1994.

Congregation for the Doctrine of the Faith. *From "Inter Insigniores" to "Ordinatio Sacerdotalis."* Washington, D.C.: United States Catholic Conference, 1998.

Bloom, Harold. *Genius: A Mosaic of One Hundred Exemplary Creative Minds.* N.Y.: Warner Books, 2002.

Dulles, S.J., Avery. "Tradition says no." *The Tablet* 249:8105 (Dec. 9, 1995).

"Ordinary Magisterium." In *Encyclopedia of Catholic Doctrine,* edited by Russell Shaw. Huntington, Ind.: Our Sunday Visitor Publishing, 1997.

Buckner, Christopher M. "Sacrament." In *Encyclopedia of Catholic Doctrine,* edited by Russell Shaw. Huntington, Ind.: Our Sunday Visitor Publishing, 1997.

Weigel, George. *The Truth of Catholicism: Ten Controversies Explored.* N.Y.: Harper Collins, 2001.

Ruether, Rosemary Radford. *Womanguides: Readings Toward a Feminist Theology.* Boston: Beacon Press, 1985.

The Praiseofglory.com website provides a page of interesting excerpts on the issue of the all-male priesthood beginning with excerpts from John Paul II's Apostolic Letter *Mulieris Dignitatem* (On the Dignity and Vocation of Women), followed by excerpts by the great Catholic theologian Hans Urs von Balthasar, by the great Anglican apologist and writer C.S. Lewis, and by Eastern Orthodox theologian Fr. Alexander Schmemann. All are available at http://praiseofglory.com/bridegroom.htm/. The *Catechism* treats the issue at section 1577, but in reality the entire article on the Sacrament of Holy Orders is essential background reading, especially sections 1544 to 1549. These sections set forth the "two participations in the one priesthood of Christ": the baptismal priesthood that includes all Christians, male and female, and the ministerial or hierarchical priesthood which is reserved for males only (Sections 1546, 1547). Section 1548 presents the role of the priest as acting in the person of Christ. But in my view the most eloquent affirmation of the all-male priesthood is Section 1120 of the *Catechism,* although it does not explicitly mention the issue of gender, because it discusses how the ordained minister "ties the liturgical action . . . to the words and actions of Christ, the source and foundation of the sacraments."

Chapter Five: Peter, the First Bishop of Rome

Jones, O.P., David Albert. "Was there a bishop of Rome in the first century?" *New Blackfriars* 80 (No. 937) (March 1999).
Sullivan, S.J., Francis A. *From Apostles to Bishops: The Development of the Episcopacy in the Early Church.* N.Y.: Newman Press, 2001.

Brown, S.S., Raymond E. "*Episkope* and *Episkopos:* The New Testament Evidence." *Theological Studies* 41 (1980).

Brown, S.S., Raymond E. *An Introduction to the New Testament.* N.Y.: Doubleday, 1997.

Richardson, Cyril C., ed. *Early Christian Fathers.* N.Y.: Simon & Schuster, 1996 ed.

Tillard, O.P., J.M.R. *The Bishop of Rome.* Wilmington, Del.: Michael Glazier, Inc., 1983.

Wills, Garry. *Why I am a Catholic.* N.Y.: Houghton Mifflin, 2002.

The relevant sections of the *Catechism* include: 552, 553, 765, 880-886. These sections focus on Peter and on the Pope as the successor of Peter, along with the other bishops as successors of the apostles.

Conclusion

Vigneron, Bishop Allen. "The New Evangelization and the Teaching of Philosophy." In *The Two Wings of Catholic Thought: Essays on Fides et ratio,* edited by David Foster & Joseph Koterski, S.J., pp. 99-108. Catholic University of America Press, 2003.

In Section 854, the *Catechism* speaks eloquently of "inculturation" as part of the missionary endeavor. This section should be read as referring not only to historically non-Christian lands but also to the post-Christian societies of Europe and North America.

Index of Names and Topics

(When a topic is the subject of an entire chapter, the chapter is indicated along with the page where that chapter begins.)

Abortion

> Legal reasoning (Ch. 1), 22
> Scientific evidence against (Ch. 1), 11

Augustine of Hippo, 46

Birth control/contraception (Ch. 3), 43

Bishop, first century definition of, 76

Bridegroom/Bride image, 53

Casey v. Planned Parenthood, 22, 25, 29

Catechism of the Catholic Church, 8

Chastity (Ch. 2), 32

Clement of Rome, 66

Communism, 41

Conscience, 42

Cyprian, St., 51

Democrats, 34

Dred Scott decision, 21

Dulles, Avery Cardinal, 49, 54, 58

Dworkin, Ronald, 11, 13

Eastern Orthodox, 56, 62

Embryology and fetology, 15, 17

Eucharist, 62

Evangelicals, 56, 62

Genesis, 38

Goldberg, Bernard, 33

Heidegger, 6

Infallibility, 54

John Paul II, 32, 34, 37, 38, 43, 50, 54, 59, 63

Jones, O.P., David Albert, 64

King James (Authorized) Version of the Bible, 71, 74

Magisterium, 58

Magisterium, extraordinary & ordinary, 59

Marian profile, 61

Mono-episcopacy, 68

Nathanson, Dr. Bernard, 12, 14, 15

Nuptial meaning of the body, 38

Nuptial mystery, 61

Ortega y Gasset, 5, 6, 7

Paul of Tarsus, 77

Paul VI, 47, 54, 55

Peter, first bishop of Rome (Ch. 5), 64

Petrine profile, 61

Presbyters, 71

Priesthood, All-Male (Ch. 4), 48

Roe v. Wade, 18, 22, 23, 26, 28, 29, 30

Ruether, Rosemary, 63

Sacramental matter, 60

Scandals, clergy, 57

Smith, Janet, 44

Sullivan, S.J., Francis, 64, 67

Supreme Court, U.S., 19, 20, 22

Theology of the Body, 34, 37

Vatican II, 6, 38, 45, 46

Vigneron, Bishop Allen, 80

Weigel, George, 61

Wills, Garry, 64

Women's priestly ordination, six arguments

against, 59

Index of Theological Sources

Scriptural sources (in canonical order):

Genesis (general reference), p. 38

Luke 19:44, pp. 70, 75

John 21:15-17, pp. 70, 74, 75

Acts 1:20, pp. 70, 71

Acts 5:1-6, p. 73

Acts 20:28, p. 70

Galatians 2:9, p. 77

Philippians 1:1, pp. 70, 76

1 Timothy 3:1, pp. 70, 71

1 Timothy 3:2, pp. 68, 70, 71.

1 Timothy 5:17, p. 71

Titus 1:7, pp. 68, 70

Titus 1:7-15, p. 73

Hebrews 12:15, pp. 70, 73

1 Peter 2:12, pp. 70, 75

1 Peter 2:25, pp. 68, 70, 73, 74

1 Peter 5:1, p. 72

1 Peter 5:2, pp. 70, 72, 74

1 Peter 5:4, p. 76

Magisterial sources (in chronological order):

Second Vatican Council, *Gaudium et Spes (Pastoral Constitution of the Church in the Modern World)*, promulgated by Paul VI on Dec. 7, 1965, pp. 45, 46

Paul VI, Encyclical Letter *Humanae Vitae (Of Human Life)*, July 25, 1968, pp. 47, 49

Congregation for the Doctrine of the Faith, Declaration *Inter Insigniores (Regarding the Question of the Admission of Women to Ministerial Priesthood)*, approved, confirmed, and ordered published by Paul VI on Oct. 15, 1976, pp. 50-54

John Paul II, Weekly General Audiences on the Theology of the Body (Sept. 1979-Nov. 1984), pp. 37-39, 53

John Paul II, Apostolic Letter *Ordinatio Sacerdotalis (On Reserving Priestly Ordination to Men Alone)*, May 22, 1994, pp. 50, 55

John Paul II, Encyclical Letter *Evangelium Vitae (The Gospel of Life)*, Mar. 25, 1995, p. 44

Patristic sources:

First Letter of Clement to the Corinthians, p. 66

Reference sources:

Russell Shaw, ed., *Encyclopedia of Catholic Doctrine* (1997), p. 59

Printed in the United Kingdom
by Lightning Source UK Ltd.
108127UKS00001B/232